Teaching Racial Literacy

Teaching Racial Literacy

Reflective Practices for Critical Writing

Mara Lee Grayson

ROWMAN & LITTLEFIELD
Lanham • Boulder • New York • London

Published by Rowman & Littlefield
A wholly owned subsidiary of The Rowman & Littlefield Publishing Group, Inc.
4501 Forbes Boulevard, Suite 200, Lanham, Maryland 20706
www.rowman.com

Unit A, Whitacre Mews, 26-34 Stannary Street, London SE11 4AB

British Library Cataloguing in Publication Information Available

Library of Congress Cataloging-in-Publication Data

Names: Grayson, Mara Lee, 1985- author.
Title: Teaching racial literacy : reflective practices for critical writing /
    Mara Lee Grayson.
Description: Lanham : Rowman & Littlefield, [2018] | Includes bibliographical
    references and index.
Identifiers: LCCN 2017048315 (print) | LCCN 2017061750 (ebook) | ISBN
    9781475836622 (electronic) | ISBN 9781475836608 (cloth : alk. paper) |
    ISBN 9781475836615 (pbk. : alk. paper)
Subjects: LCSH: English language—Rhetoric—Study and teaching
    (Higher)—United States. | Anti-racism—Study and teaching. |
    Discrimination in higher education—United States.
Classification: LCC PE1404.G73 2018 (ebook) | LCC PE1404.G73 2018 (print) |
    DDC 808/.042071173—dc23
LC record available at https://lccn.loc.gov/2017048315

Printed in the United States of America

To the legacy of activism in my mother's family and to my father, who taught me that the meandering journey is just as beautiful as the direct path and that art, in all its forms, is the lifeblood that makes us human.

Martin Kornberg

1938–2011

Contents

Acknowledgments

Foremost, my utmost thanks to the students I have taught. Over the years, you have confided in me, challenged me, calmed me, and confirmed my belief that the heart of this scholarship is my commitment to you.

This book would not exist were it not for Rowman & Littlefield acquisitions editor Sarah Jubar, who found me amid a convention center full of English educators and immediately recognized the necessity and timeliness of this work.

Thanks to Meaghan Brewer and Laurie McMillan for their feedback on the manuscript's earliest draft and to Rachel Golland and Brice Particelli for sharing their classroom practices and allowing me to share those practices with readers.

There are never enough words to thank the scholars with whom I have been fortunate enough to study and whose work has paved the way for my own. Sheridan Blau, Ernest Morrell, and Yolanda Sealey-Ruiz, I remain indebted to you.

Finally, heartfelt personal thanks to my husband Aleksandr Doyban. Alex, your love, support, and confidence in me—even when my own confidence is waning—mean more than I can express on this page. Я тебя люблю.

Introduction

Halfway through the fall of 2013, I administered midterm essay exams to the twenty-two students enrolled in the second-semester First-Year Composition (FYC) course I was teaching at a public community college in New York City. The English department mandated that the course, officially titled Writing through Literature, employ literary texts as jumping-off points for critical writing. Instructors were also required to teach three distinct literary genres.

At the time, most of my colleagues divided the semester into units on fiction, poetry, and drama. Until October 2013, I had structured my course the same way. The midterm I gave that month required students to answer in essay form an analytical question pertaining to one of the short stories or poems we had read and discussed as a class. In these essays, however, my students had not demonstrated the abilities I was confident they possessed to critically analyze a literary text.

Figuring a curricular shift was in order, I brought to our next class session the lyrics to "Norwegian Wood" by the Beatles. I had hoped that the brevity of this lyrical text would encourage the class to focus intensively on individual moments within. Because songs are compact forms intended to evoke an immediate response, they express "within a few minutes a range of emotions and ideas" that make them ideal for textual analysis in the classroom.[1]

I chose this particular song for a few reasons, one of which was its relative obscurity, at least among the students in my classroom. Despite the popularity of the Beatles, when I asked my students if they knew "Norwegian Wood," only one student was familiar with the song. This was an important criterion in its selection, as it allowed for distance in analysis and lessened—though it would be impossible to eliminate, given the Beatles' notoriety—the preconceived notions students brought to the text. One lesser, though not inconsequential, reason for starting with "Norwegian Wood" was my personal familiarity with and fondness for the song. While I ordinarily enjoy the process of meaning making alongside my students, I felt most comfortable venturing into new territory with a familiar companion by my side.

The most significant factor in my selection of this particular song was that its lyrics told a story. While song lyrics are frequently compared to poetry, what I have come to term narrative song lyrics (from here on NSL) far more resemble short stories set to music and utilize traditional techniques of storytelling, like plot, character, setting, and conflict, just to name a few. Once I had distributed the lyrics of "Norwegian Wood" and a list of six questions for students to consider, I set three objectives for the lesson: (1) Students should be able to identify the literary elements and devices we had discussed earlier in the semester, including character, plot, and point of view; (2) students should extrapolate from the text to answer questions; and (3) students should support their arguments using specific examples.

I broke students into groups of three and four; in these groups, they worked together to answer the questions posed. The subsequent discussions were livelier and the students more engaged than I had seen yet that semester. In one group, two students offered differing perspectives on the relationship between the characters in the story song. In another group, a student, who had until then been very quiet in class discussion, explained in layman's terms the meaning of *meter* to one of his group mates. In a third, students debated the significance of the song's title.

Even when they disagreed on the interpretation of the material, the students were thorough and expressive in their attempts to justify their individual perspectives. They backed up their ideas with quotes and drew logical conclusions based on textual evidence. These were all areas in which the students had had trouble on their first set of essays and on the midterm exam.

As students became more comfortable with the language of literary analysis, I brought in other song lyrics, all of which possessed a common set of characteristics: There was a plot, which consisted of a clear beginning, middle, and end; a setting was established, either directly or implicitly; characters were identified and developed; and literary devices and figurative language, such as imagery, simile, and metaphor, were employed. These new NSL texts included story songs by Bruce Springsteen, Tracy Chapman, and Eminem. For this first foray into the NSL curriculum, I selected songs with literary elements that were clear but not overt or simplistic; all had some level of ambiguity to encourage students to look closely at the text. Lyrics were read primarily as written texts, though songs were played following initial textual analysis to allow students to appreciate the "atmosphere of the music" and consider how their instrumental elements contribute to the songs' meanings.[2]

Then something strange happened. Without my urging, discussions of NSL texts turned into conversations about the class system in the United States, Barack Obama's presidency, racial imbalances within the U.S. justice system, and the stigmas associated with collecting food stamps or welfare. I had introduced this curriculum as an attempt to bring my students closer to the language of literary criticism; it transmuted over the course of the semester into an attempt to observe and encourage the open, direct dialogue about race, ethnicity, and class that only became apparent with the introduction of song lyrics.

More amazingly, students' written work began to improve. Their reading responses were simultaneously more personal and more analytical (which showed me they were more engaged in the material), and on their final papers, they effectively connected their analyses of these NSL texts to personal and societal problems they had witnessed or experienced in their own lives outside of school.

This phenomenon struck me as rather peculiar, as the stories my students had read during the first half of the semester—works by Junot Díaz and Raymond Carver, among others—seemed to lend themselves much more to such critical discussions, particularly with regard to race, ethnicity, and socioeconomic class. Yet, while the students seemed to comprehend those stories, reading and discussing them had not led to such discourse. The NSL curriculum, however, did.

Moreover, students seemed to care about the coursework. Attendance was consistent from week to week (which was not common at the community college). Most students participated in conversation. And, while the papers they submitted at the end of the semester were not flawless in terms of structure or grammar, it was clear in their writing that they had critically engaged with the texts they had read. The story song genre seemed to both pique student interest and introduce critical discourse on matters of race and racism.

I began to wonder: Could this curriculum help improve not only student engagement in the classroom but also their understanding of social (in)justice? If so, what other curricula could engage young people in such critical discussions?

THE CURRICULUM IN CONTEXT

At the same time that I addressed this question in the often too narrow world of academia, the United States saw renewed attention to racial dynamics in the arenas of politics, popular culture, higher education, and criminal justice. In the second half of 2014, a string of police killings of unarmed Black boys and men, including Eric Garner in Staten Island, New York, in July; Michael Brown in Ferguson, Missouri, in August; and twelve-year-old Tamir Rice in Cleveland, Ohio, in November ignited protests and riots across the country, which only intensified after the officers responsible for the deaths of Garner and Brown failed to be indicted.

Many of these protests were organized by or affiliated with Black Lives Matter, an activist organization that originated as part of a Facebook post, arose to prominence as a legitimate political movement, and revitalized youth and grassroots activism.[3] It has also led to backlash, as heard in the reactionary slogans "All Lives Matter" and "Blue Lives Matter," the former of which antiracism activists have seen as racist, diversionary, and emblematic of our country's cultural "empathy gap"[4] and the latter of which has been labelled as a false equivalency.

College campuses, too, became sites of racial struggle. Throughout the fall of 2015, acts of racism and discrimination plagued the University of Missouri, Columbia, including offensive images taped to dormitory doors and threats to Black students posted on social media. Students' frustrations with the university's failure to act on these threats in a timely matter resulted in highly publicized protests, a hunger strike, a football team boycott, and the resignation of the university's president. At Princeton University, students conducted sit-ins on campus to advocate for a renaming of the Woodrow Wilson School of Public and International Affairs due to the former U.S. and Princeton University president's support of racial segregation.

Neither the 2008 election nor 2012 reelection of Black-identifying American president Barack Obama succeeded in ushering in the "potential postracial moment" initially promised.[5] Critics have pointed out that postracial rhetoric exploited Barack Obama's election in attempts to eliminate historicity from discourse on racism, thereby maintaining the inequitable social structures of American society. While some have argued that Obama himself campaigned on a postracial platform,[6] the eight years of his presidency were plagued by renewed racial tensions across the United States and, with the involvement of social media, increased awareness of American racial inequity.

By 2016, Donald J. Trump, a billionaire real estate mogul with no political experience, had launched a divisive presidential campaign that brought questions of immigration, the White working class, sexual assault, and the entire political establishment to the forefront of American discourse. Buoyed by promises to "make America great again" and despite losing the popular vote to Democratic candidate Hillary Clinton, at close to 4 a.m. on November 9, 2016, Trump gained the electoral votes needed to be elected president. Protests and petitions sprang up all over the country in hopes of pressuring electors to vote against their obligations to state to prevent Trump from ascending to the most powerful position in U.S. government. These protests were unsuccessful, however, and in January 2017, Trump was inaugurated as the forty-fifth president of the United States of America.

Trump's election only exacerbated the racial tensions that already existed on high school and college campuses. Swastikas were found painted on the campuses of the New School and the State University of New York at Geneseo, and references to "nigger lynching" circulated on social media at the University of Pennsylvania. While the problematic false color blindness that prevailed during the eight years of the Obama administration necessitated direct, verbal discussion of the systemic racism and racialism that undergird American life, this new sociopolitical era demands an even more rigorous approach to addressing race, racism, and social (in)justice.

RACIAL LITERACY IN THE CLASSROOM

Racial literacy, a collection of skills and behaviors that allow individuals to "probe the existence of racism and examine the effects of race and institutionalized systems on their experiences and representation in US society,"[7] is vital in a contemporary American society that professes meritocracy and postracialism yet where racial inequality continues to give rise to fear, violence, and inequity.

Because racial literacy requires us to develop a cache of discursive tools with which to critically read and respond to particular situations and broader societal practices, as well as to investigate the rhetorical practices and power of the long-standing hegemonic infrastructure of American life, I argue that there is no venue better fitted to the development of racial literacy than the classroom. But how do we facilitate such discourse? And to what ends do we facilitate these conversations? Equally important, how might the discursive practices of racial literacy contribute to student engagement and achievement in the classroom?

Racial literacy is not merely about understanding or talking about race—it is, in fact, a specific framework that can be used to interrogate race and racism (I discuss the particulars of that framework more fully in chapter 1). That said, the significance of the word *literacy* cannot be understated. Racial literacy demands not only that we develop a multilayered understanding of the function(s) of race in society but also that we learn to read individual situations for the ways in which they represent, reinforce, or resist systemic injustice. We must also consider how the language we use and the writing we produce is situated and racialized, regardless of our intention. In addition to making space to interrogate race and racism, a racial literacy curriculum can introduce students to foundational concepts of literacy and rhetoric, such as authorial positionality, language choice, representation, critical media literacy, textual analysis, and audience. Put simply, a strong education in racial literacy is a strong education in literacy.

WHAT TO EXPECT

This book provides an overview of the racial literacy framework in composition instruction, as well as practical strategies for implementation. Drawing on a three-year ethnographic teacher research project, I offer curriculum suggestions and teacher resources designed to help composition instructors introduce to students the tools of racial literacy with the goals of increasing student engagement, developing awareness of structural inequity and discursive modes with which to respond to social injustice, and improving student writing.

Chapter 1 serves as an introduction to the framework of racial literacy and its connection to the practices of critical writing and literacy instruction. In this chapter, I address racial literacy as both a critical lens for the understanding of race and related variables and as a curricular goal for the courses we teach. Chapter 2 invites instructors to consider the role of racial literacy in their own classrooms. Instructors are guided through three steps of the planning process: (1) considering one's own positionality and relationship to questions of race and racism, (2) determining the connections between racial literacy and the goals of their particular classes, and

(3) designing curricula that speak to both the goals of the course and the needs of the students in the classroom.

Chapter 3 addresses text selection in the racial literacy classroom. Taking into account the digital literacies and multimodality of the twenty-first-century classroom, I address the rationale for the particular texts teachers choose to incorporate into the racial literacy curriculum, as well as the logistical considerations behind those selections. Chapter 4 describes one text-based approach to the racial literacy curriculum. Drawing from my own experience using narrative song lyrics as literary texts, I discuss the use of the NSL curriculum to encourage critical discussion of race and textual representation.

Chapter 5 addresses one of the most significant yet also one of the most difficult components of teaching racial literacy: the emotional weight of the curriculum. In this chapter, I discuss the role of emotion in racial literacy, provide an overview the types of emotional responses teachers can expect from students, and offer strategies to help instructors manage students' emotions safely and equitably. Chapter 6 more deeply explores the concept of individual positionality, not only with regards to matters of race, racism, and racialism, but also in relation to questions of authorship and textual representation.

Chapter 7 considers the silences that prevail in conversations around race, particularly in the writing classroom. I provide tools through which instructors can analyze the significance of what is unsaid and develop lessons around those gaps. In chapter 8, I consider the role of racial literacy and writing to build bridges between the classroom and the community. In other words, how can students use the writing they do inside the classroom to interrogate broader inequities—and, most importantly, advocate for change on campus and in the community?

Chapters 3 through 8 include two additional features: a *teacher resource*, a unit of instruction or activity instructors can bring into the classroom; and an *instructional strategy*, a pedagogical approach (though not necessarily a tangible activity) that instructors can use to help students work through course material. Excerpts from in-class discussions and written work by students studying racial literacy curricula are included in each chapter to provide readers with a sense of the possible outcomes of teaching—and teaching with—racial literacy.

Chapter 9 is geared specifically toward the secondary instructor. Here I offer additional suggestions that should be considered when working with students under age eighteen, as well as strategies for cooperating with parents and administrators. Finally, at the end of the book, I provide a list of additional resources for teachers—and students—of racial literacy.

A NOTE ON THE TERMINOLOGY USED IN THIS BOOK

I use the term *racism* throughout this book to refer to a "system of advantage"[8] that "creates or reproduces structures of domination based on essentialist categories of race."[9] While individual situations of discrimination are evidence of larger structural inequities, I use the term *racism* to refer to the broader system of racial hierarchy and oppression. I further draw on a critical race theory that maintains that racism is not out of the ordinary but instead the normal way of doing things in society.

Some researchers of race relations and racial identity formation in education have chosen not to capitalize racial identifiers, such as *black* and *white*, in order to "minimize the notion of racial categories as immutable entities."[10] I have chosen, however, to capitalize the terms *Black* and *White* (and *Brown*) throughout this book in order to emphasize their assignment as social classifications rather than innate biological characteristics.

I have also chosen the term *minoritized* to refer to non-White populations because I believe that it best conveys the active, systematic oppression by which non-White populations are positioned as minorities in a White-dominated society.

Race and *ethnicity* are two additional terms found in this book. The following explanations are in no way intended as definitions of what are at times contested and controversial terms but are instead offered to establish a foundation for the shorthand readers can find in the pages that follow. I use the term *ethnicity* to denote the group with which an individual shares a common descent. In sociological and social science scholarship, the term typically emphasizes shared cultural community rather than solely biology.[11]

While I interrogate definitions of race throughout the book, note that, when I employ this term as a mode of classification, I am referring to one or more of the terms officially classified as races on the United States Census: White; Black or African American; Asian; American Indian or Alaska Native; and Hawaiian Native or Other Pacific Islander.[12] Regardless of how problematic these categorizations may be from sociological and sociocultural perspectives, they are, as the official options in use, structurally significant to an understanding of race as a social and political classification.

When I present anecdotes and excerpts from student writing, I have tried for the most part to stay true to students' uses of terms, so that if a student has racially self-identified with an ethnic term rather than a governmentally sanctioned racial term, for example, I honor that student's selected identifiers. I at times address disjunctions between student speech or writing and social or scholarly terminology or both, but I believe that, as educators and teacher-researchers, we have a duty to honor the voices of the students in our classrooms.

NOTES

1. Robert McParland, "A Sound Education: Popular Music in the College Composition Classroom," in *Teaching in the Pop Culture Zone: Using Popular Culture in the Composition Classroom*, eds. Allison D. Smith, Trixie G. Smith, and Rebecca Bobbitt (Boston: Wadsworth, 2009), 102.

2. Ibid., 103.

3. Jelani Cobb, "The Matter of Black Lives," *New Yorker* 92, no. 5 (2016): 34.

4. L-Mani S. Viney, "Here's Why It Hurts When People Say 'All Lives Matter,'" *Vanity Fair*, July 19, 2016.

5. Marc P. Johnston-Guerrero, "The Meanings of Race Matter: College Students Learning about Race in a Not-So-Postracial Era," *American Educational Research Journal* 53, no. 4 (2016): 820.

6. See Tim Wise, *Colorblind: The Rise of Post-Racial Politics and the Retreat from Racial Equity* (San Francisco: City Lights, 2010).

7. Yolanda Sealey-Ruiz, "Building Racial Literacy in First-Year Composition," *Teaching English in the Two-Year College* 40, no. 4 (2013): 386.

8. David T. Wellman, *Portraits of White Racism*, 2nd ed. (Cambridge: Cambridge University Press, 1993).

9. Michael Omi and Howard Winant, *Racial Formation in the United States: From the 1960s to the 1990s*, 2nd ed. (New York: Routledge, 1994), 71.

10. Kristen A. Renn, "Patterns of Situational Identity among Biracial and Multiracial College Students," *Review of Higher Education* 23, no. 4 (2000). See also Marc P. Johnston-Guerrero, "Meanings."

11. Ann Morning, "Ethnic Classification in Global Perspective: A Cross-National Survey of the 2000 Census Round," *United Nations.org*, last modified August 10, 2005, https://un stats.un.org/unsd/demographic/sconcerns/popchar/Morning.pdf.

12. United States Census Bureau, "Race—About," *Census.gov*, last modified July 8, 2013, http://www.census.gov/topics/population/race/about.html.

1

Racial Literacy and the College Composition Classroom

"I'm sick of talking about race!"

These are the words of a former colleague who, having inquired as to the research I was conducting, dramatically sighed and informed me that she planned to never again discuss race with her students. Race had nothing to do with composition, she insisted, especially in the twenty-first century.[1]

The writing teacher is in a unique position to shape her classroom as a workshop of sorts for the larger world her students inhabit. By learning to identify and critique the ideas and underlying ideologies of literary and rhetorical texts, students are then able to apply those techniques to the social, cultural, and political events they encounter outside the classroom.

Unfortunately, many educators and educational administrators still see questions of culture and societal ideology—particularly with regards to race, a subject of discussion fraught with tensions and silences—as outside the scope of our curricula. With the myriad pressures instructors face when designing curricula and implementing instruction, incorporating race and racism may seem like an added burden that would be simpler to not address at all. After all, race talk is not easy to initiate or navigate—and with all the other pressures placed on today's teachers, some teachers would rather just avoid it.

Given the significant position race has occupied and, more importantly, continues to occupy in our society, we cannot and should not pretend to be apolitical. To attempt to isolate literacy from its sociological and cultural influences is to create a false vacuum of our discipline. At a time when Writing in the Disciplines and Writing across the Curriculum courses make up a considerable part of university English department offerings, this vacuum is quite obviously illogical. It is also tantamount to an act of intellectual violence against our students. By painting a half-picture of composition and eliminating context and relevancy from our instruction, we leave young people with a set of skills yet little understanding of their usage and potential—for oppression, liberation, or both—outside the classroom.

CULTURE, LITERACY, AND THE CLASSROOM

Historically, both the definition of literacy and related instructional practices have been inextricably linked to surrounding social and cultural ideologies, practices, and values. These values determine how and when letters might be written, the type of stories that are read or told to children, and how and by whom official forms and documents are interpreted or completed. Literacy education has always shifted in response to the needs of the students in the classroom and the broader needs of the society. While explicit classroom discussion of race is a rather new development in English education, the fields of English and English education have always responded, often implicitly, to the social and cultural diversity of the student population.

In the United States, immigration has long been one of the driving forces behind changes in literacy curricula. Faced with the continuous influx of various immigrant populations, American public education has systematically equipped—or denied—students with the skills needed for assimilation (and acculturation) into American society. In the early years of American independence, the role of schools in promoting active citizenship and republican values was widely celebrated, both nationally and within local communities. However, these lofty goals were largely unmet through instructional praxis, to the extent that one must question their initial legitimacy.

At this time, classical instruction defined the pedagogical paradigm of literacy education. Heavily influenced by Platonic philosophy and European instructional models, classical instruction relied largely on imitation, memorization, and oral recitation. These pedagogical practices were directly linked both to classical conceptions of morality, beauty, and knowledge and to contemporary educational goals, primarily the assimilation of poor and immigrant students (and those of otherwise nondominant home cultures) and the transmission of those nationally held ideologies. In order for the immigrant child to be Americanized, it was imperative that he be taught what is good, beautiful, and important in American culture. The modes of instruction employed, however, were problematic for students with nondominant language practices and little experience living and attending school in the United States.

Continually increasing immigration, scientific developments, and the industrial economy of the early twentieth century mediated the shift from classical to progressive education. Pioneered by John Dewey and further developed with a consideration of new educational psychology, Progressive Era reform imagined education as a key means for social progress. With the goal to provide the "skills, knowledge, and social attitudes required for urbanized commercial and industrial society,"[2] instructional practices included experience-based writing; the introduction of popular culture texts, such as film and radio; and an emphasis on functional applications of literacy, such as library techniques and business writing.

By the 1960s, ethnographic research had begun to influence not only the way scholars and educators viewed literacy but also how literacy practices and classroom pedagogy came to be investigated. Educators, sociologists, and anthropologists began to conduct research from within cultural communities, exploring the social and cultural situated-ness of literacy practices. Literacy research came to be seen as contextual, taking into account the particular uses of literacy within a particular society. Sociocultural approaches to literacy research and new theories of literacy as a cultural practice encouraged pedagogies that attempted to bring students' outside literacy practices into the classroom.

More broadly, these scholarly advances, along with open-enrollment policies in public colleges that increased the presence of traditionally underrepresented populations (including Blacks, Latino/as, and women) in the classroom, required educators and policy makers to expand their notions of literacy and recognize the validity of out-of-school language and literacy practices.

Attempts at Equity in Composition Instruction

In 1972, the Conference on College Composition and Communication (CCCC) passed a resolution on Students' Right to Their Own Language. The resolution, which affirmed the "students' right to their own patterns and varieties of language—the dialects of their nurture or whatever dialects in which they find their own identity and style,"[3] accounted for regional dialect but was largely responsive to the African American population and civil rights era reform. While the CCCC attempted to persuade the National Council of Teachers of English (NCTE) to adopt the resolution, NCTE passed a less progressive version of the resolution in 1974, emphasizing that, while spoken dialect should be recognized, students should still be taught to write with the standard conventions of what was then called edited American English (or what others have come to term White mainstream English and standard American English).

Around the same time, Brazilian educator and philosopher Paulo Freire suggested that literacy instruction should focus more on helping those who cannot read to better interpret the world around them and come to understand their own roles not as illiterates outside of society but oppressed people within that society. The establishment of a *critical consciousness* with which to read and analyze the world in which one exists became integral to our understanding of literacy as a far greater endeavor than adopting the skills of decoding and reproducing the written word.

Late-twentieth-century approaches to race and diversity in the classroom included multicultural education and culturally relevant pedagogy. Five tenets of multicultural education included (1) *content integration*, the inclusion of diverse people and perspectives into the curriculum; (2) *knowledge construction*, the identification of one's own frames of reference and assumptions about the world; (3) *equity pedagogy*, the use of diverse teaching methods to best reach a wider range of students; (4) *prejudice reduction*, the aim to help students develop positive racial attitudes; and (5) *empowering school culture*, the encouragement of equitable education on a larger scale than the individual classroom.

Despite the intentions of multicultural education, many educators believed its implementations—usually limited to content integration—were too simplistic to achieve equitable ends.[4] Because forays into nondominant cultures without an explicitly antiracist ideology can serve as little more than voyeurism, multicultural pedagogy often failed to provide adequate understanding of the values and norms of other cultures and may have reinforced hierarchies among dominant and minoritized groups.

Culturally relevant and culturally responsive pedagogies include students' culture in the classroom without exoticizing it as *other*. Scholarship on culturally relevant pedagogy originally emphasized the teaching of Black and African American students but expanded to address the education of other minoritized racial and ethnic groups, including Asian Americans, Latin Americans, and Native Americans. Teachers employing culturally relevant pedagogy have encouraged their students to bring to class materials from home that relate to the curriculum, such as rap songs during a poetry unit; invited parents into the classroom to share a skill or tradition, which students then researched and wrote about; and allowed students to use their "home language" while learning academic discourse in the classroom.[5]

To prevent these practices from being too individualistic, culturally relevant pedagogy emphasized historical context; encouraged students to reach out in their communities, such as by writing letters to their congresspersons; and employed multiple perspectives on relevant issues. A culturally responsive classroom highlights the potent resources already available in communities of color; such an orientation not only honors students' out-of-school practices but also highlights the educational assets rather than deficits of minoritized communities.

A great deal of educational research in recent years has addressed the necessity of equitable, culturally relevant curricula for students in homogeneously Black public-school settings. However, it is a mistake (and an essentialist conflation) to associate racially cognizant pedagogies with Black students. Race and racism affect everyone, whether everyone realizes or chooses to acknowledge it or not. While the institutions and ideologies that define American education were conceived through a White Euro-American framework (and have therefore been best fit for an increasingly limited population of students), it is important to continue not only to resist White hegemony but also to question it—and invite our students to critique its workings.

Race Talk in the Classroom

Even if we were to accept the flawed argument that composition itself has nothing to do with race, we cannot deny that the *teaching* of composition (like the broader field of English education) is concerned with questions of race, racialization, racism, antiracism, and social justice. Race has factored, implicitly or explicitly, into research and scholarship on reading and text selection, remediation, student experience and identity, form and structure, campus politics, and dialect and language variation in the classroom. Critical writing demands attention be paid not only to ideas but also to the rhetorical and discursive construction and explication of those ideas; simply put, it's not only *what* we say but also *how* we say it. Tasked with the responsibility of introducing students to the literacy practices of the academy, writing instructors also help make visible the processes by which ideas and ideologies are constructed, maintained, and subverted. But how?

The truth is that race talk *is* difficult. It can be uncomfortable and contentious, and often, it leaves us with more questions than answers. Attempting to facilitate conversations around race and racism without a plan or framework can be met with awkwardness, negativity, or even silence.

In the classroom, the racial literacy framework provides a critical lens through which to view race and race talk as well as the goal of curricula developed within that framework. With this framework in mind, instructors can develop curricula that introduce students both to the social functions of race and the ways in which language can serve to maintain or reshape racial ideologies.

THE RACIAL LITERACY FRAMEWORK

The framework of racial literacy emerged simultaneously from the fields of sociology and legal studies and quickly made its way into education, factoring into scholarship on college admissions, administrative policy, and teacher education. Racial literacy is not only about understanding race—it is also a multilayered conceptual framework designed to help us do so.

France Winddance Twine's ethnographic case study of White mothers of biracial children identified three practices that comprise racial literacy, a term the author employed to theorize "parental labour as a type of anti-racist project"[6]: the provision of conceptual and discursive practices with which to understand the function(s) of race; access to Black social networks; and exposure to Black-produced media and significant symbols of Black struggles. Twine's initial conceptualization of racial literacy does not provide tools with which to address the racialized experiences of non-Black people of color, however, as does the racial literacy paradigm described by legal scholar Lani Guinier. Guinier contends that racial literacy is contextual; considers the "psychological, interpersonal, and structural dimensions" of race[7]; and "constantly interrogates the dynamic relationship among race, class, geography, gender, and other explanatory variables."[8] Racial inequities are representative of larger societal injustices that also affect other minoritized and marginalized populations.

Twine's expanded racial literacy framework provides both a broader understanding of race and a more concrete framework for the practice of racial literacy. Table 1.1 displays the characteristics and skills of the racial literacy framework in three iterations.

Table 1.1.   Characteristics and Behaviors of Racial Literacy

Guinier 2004	Twine 2004	Twine 2010
• Recognition that race, racialism, and racism are contextual • Views of race on psychological, interpersonal, and structural levels • Consideration of race as it intersects with other demographic factors, including but not limited to ethnicity, socioeconomic class, geography, and gender	• Provision of conceptual and discursive practices through which to interrogate race • Access to Black social networks • Exposure to Black-produced media and symbols of historical and cultural Black struggles	• Recognition of racism as a contemporary rather than historical problem • Consideration of the ways in which race and racism are influenced by other factors, such as class, gender, and sexuality • Understanding of the cultural value of Whiteness • Belief in the constructedness and socialization of racial identity • Development of language practices through which to discuss race, racism, and antiracism • Ability to decode race and racialism

Due in part to the framework's emphasis on discursive and decoding practices, research on racial literacy pedagogy has emerged from English and composition classrooms at all levels, from early childhood education and secondary English language arts to undergraduate composition classrooms on racially diverse campuses and racially homogeneous ones. Racial literacy in teacher education prepares new teachers to work in racially diverse environments and to interrogate how their understandings of people of different races are influenced by and representative of broader societal inequities and media stereotypes. In high school and college classrooms, students read racially charged texts, engage in problem-solving group discussions, and use reflective writing to identify and respond to racial inequity.

To develop pedagogies around the discursive practices of racial literacy, however, it is first necessary to identify those discursive practices. Though open discussion and written reflection may be a useful starting point to racial literacy in composition studies curricula, it is not enough to encourage students to write and talk about race and racism. Engaging students through classroom discussion is a significant component of a successful racial literacy curriculum, but the need for free conversation cannot be the sole justification for the implementation of racial literacy curricula in the English classroom. To explore racial literacy's relevance for the classroom, connections must be drawn between these practices and the concepts taught in composition instruction.

RACIAL LITERACY IN CRITICAL WRITING INSTRUCTION

Racial literacy is about far more than content integration or developing a theme-based writing curriculum. Very broadly, English education scholarship in the past century has defined being literate as the abilities to decode, comprehend, interpret, critique, respond to, and communicate with various types of texts. The practice of racial literacy requires students to decode race and racism, comprehend the historical and contemporary structures of institutional racism, interpret individual examples of racism and racialism, critique inequity, respond to injustice, and communicate with classmates of similar and different experiences and understandings of the world.

When students practice racial literacy, they demonstrate the literacy skills that have historically defined our field of instruction. It is important to remember that literacy is not merely an academic skill. It is integral to understanding the ways in which language and texts—printed, media, or experiential—work to maintain or challenge social hierarchies and cultural hegemony. In short, racial literacy *is* literacy.

What, then, are the integral components of a racial literacy curriculum? And how might instructors bridge the critical social awareness racial literacy encourages with the foundational skills of the writing classroom?

Exploring Individual Identity

"My identity is constantly changing. Who I am today—how I feel, what I think—may not be who I am tomorrow."

—Jayna (Puerto Rican, White)

Before individuals can consider the structural and systemic functions of race, they must first consider how they see themselves and how their conceptualizations of themselves are affected by the racial ideologies of their cultures and communities. Much of the racial literacy curriculum, therefore, deals with individual identity.

In the framework's sociological origins, racial literacy was an identity-building process by which biracial children raised by White mothers could develop a positive, antiracist Black identity. Identity development in the racial literacy classroom maintains this emphasis on positive racial identity but is intersectional, taking into account factors that, along with race, contribute to one's sense of identity as an individual and a social being and to the ways in which one approaches the racial literacy curriculum.

Some students identify more immediately with other aspects of their identities, like gender, sexuality, or religion. Others find that their out-of-school identities play a significant part in their identity development. For some, their roles as parents, children, or spouses provide a lens through which to interrogate race. Instructors in universities with large veteran populations may also have students whose military service and separation therefrom factor into how they see not only themselves but also their classmates, not to mention the social and political aspects of the racial literacy curriculum.

Individual identity and interpersonal interaction are intrinsically and inextricably intertwined. The sociological approach of *symbolic interactionism* holds that "individuals make meaning through microscale interactions with others."[9] Through this lens, students can explore the ways in which their social networks contribute to their symbolic understanding of race and identity over time. For many, the transition from high school to college may come with a significant shift in those social networks. Students are likely to encounter, possibly for the first time, peers whose backgrounds differ substantially from their own. These new encounters present new challenges in communication and understanding and require the improvement of existing interpersonal skills, as well as, perhaps, the development of new ones.

Improving Interpersonal Interactions

> "He kept asking why I was yelling at him, but I wasn't yelling. I was just really passionate about the conversation!"
>
> —Talia (White, Jewish)

Entering college expands students' social networks and increases their interaction with peers of different racial backgrounds. This interaction, however, comes with challenges that aren't only limited to differences in experience, upbringing, and beliefs. In the classroom, cross-racial interaction can be difficult because of the distinct ways individuals from different backgrounds communicate their experiences and ideas.

Communication styles differ between racial groups and typically reflect longstanding cultural ideologies. Generally speaking, Asian American communication styles emphasize subtlety and cooperation. African American communication styles, on the other hand, are generally more animated, impassioned, and direct. White American communication styles tend toward objectivity, emotional detachment, and reason. These characteristics refer to verbal language practices, as well as body language; beliefs about personal space; and paralanguage, the nonverbal vocal cues, including inflection, rate of speech, and cadence, that are also part of communication.

Communication styles also differ *among* cultural groups, and one cannot assume that, because a classmate shares his or her racial or ethnic affiliation, both parties will speak, listen, and respond in the same ways—or even make the same sense of information or ideas. For example, like African Americans, Italian and Jewish Americans (who today are generally considered racially White) tend toward affective communication styles in which an increase in vocal volume signifies passion and importance, a pattern that other White Americans (as well as Asian Americans) may misinterpret as a lack of emotional control. One's approach to discussion or debate has also been shown to be influenced by gender, geography, education, and career.

It is important to note that White students typically benefit more than their peers of color from cross-racial interactions. This is understandable to some extent, as Whites are the most racially segregated demographic with regards to residence and schooling across the United States. White students must understand that their class-mates of color are not there for their own educational benefit and must be encouraged to offer their peers as much as they are given in terms of new knowledge. Put simply, it is not the job of a person of color to teach a White person about racism. White students need to fully explore Whiteness—and share their understandings of themselves as White with their classmates of all races. A critical analysis of the cultural value of Whiteness and the resulting privileges is an integral component of the racial literacy curriculum.

The racial literacy classroom must be a space in which young people feel comfortable speaking openly about subjects that many adults find difficult to address. For this to be possible, students must learn interpersonal skills of sharing, inquiring, listening, acknowledging, and responding respectfully (see box 1.1).

BOX 1.1.   KEYS TO COMMUNICATION IN THE RACIAL LITERACY CLASSROOM

Share stories, feelings, and ideas.

Inquire about others as much as, if not more than, you speak about yourself.

Listen actively to others' stories. Avoid distractions and be aware of your body language, including posture, facial expressions, and eye contact.

Acknowledge what others have said, even if you don't understand or agree.

Respond with respect. Ask for clarification about what you don't understand, explain if and why you feel differently, and thank your peers for being open.

Talking about race isn't easy, and both instructors and students should expect occasional misunderstandings, awkward conversations, and feelings of discomfort. This isn't necessarily a problem—it is an opportunity for racial literacy skill building. By inviting students to examine their own dynamics with their peers, instructors can model the classroom as a microcosm of sorts for the larger worlds their students inhabit.

Addressing Structural and Systemic Inequity

> "The fact that we're aware about it and we feel a certain way about it negatively—it could lead to something. It doesn't have to be a protest or anything, as long as you're aware. Like knowledge is power."
>
> —Yasmin (Colombian)

Racial literacy curricula must be explicitly antiracist. It is not enough to teach tolerance, as multicultural education emphasized, or even appreciation of others' cultures

Table 1.2. Discursive Practices of Racial Literacy

Speech Act	Definition	Function	Student Voices	Related Rhetorical Concept(s)
Sharing	Sharing a personal experience, anecdote, or emotional reaction connected to material being discussed	To make sense of material through identification with subject matter, another person, text, or character To provide support for an expressed opinion or interpretation	"But it's not easy, though. Like, my dad, I grew up without my dad. I'm gonna share this . . ." "I have a son. He's Black. So when I see cops are killing kids who are unarmed—what do I do as a mother?" "Because I have dealt with heartbreak, I feel like I can relate." "I feel you."	*Positionality:* Sharing encourages reflection on the factors that have influenced one's relationship to content. *Authorial Choice:* Sharing encourages students to be selective about how, what, and when they share. *Relevance:* Sharing helps students see how broad societal ideologies relate to individual lives and situations.
Labeling	Self-identifying or identifying others based on race, ethnicity, language, class, or geography	To refer to a person or group of persons To interrogate the validity of a spoken label	"I don't even like saying Black people. It's Brown." "They're hicks! They're country."	*Situated Language:* Focus on word choice encourages students to consider the situatedness of language, including word origin and connotation. *Authorial Choice* (with regards to diction)

Confronting Stereotypes	Employing, identifying, questioning or challenging others' beliefs or assumptions about a group based on race, ethnicity, class, gender, or geography	To challenge the validity of another's assumption To understand the context behind the use and development of stereotypes	"But what about lifestyle? That's just their lifestyle." "I think that we have that idea of the country because that's what we see on television or in stories." "Don't speak for all of us."	*Critical Thinking:* Attempting to understand the origins of stereotypes helps students recognize the need to look beneath the surface and even conduct research in order to find explanations and solve problems. *Textual Representation:* Confronting media and textual stereotypes helps students see the constructedness of fictional elements like characterization, narration, and perspective.
Hedging	Prefacing or following a statement with a condition, clarification, or apology	To prevent others from misunderstanding or taking offense at a subsequent or preceding utterance To assuage guilt following an inflammatory statement	"Like, I don't judge nobody, but . . ." "I don't want to be offensive for any of the stuff I'm gonna say . . ." "I mean, to be honest."	*Situated Language* *Audience:* Anticipating listener reaction encourages students to consider the rhetorical relationship between writer and reader. *Authorial Voice and Tone:* Hedging encourages awareness of voice and tone in argumentation.

or one's own racial identity; racial literacy must emphasize critical awareness of the systemic racism that necessitates such curricula. Moreover, classroom practices must move students to consider their role in antiracist action. This may feel like a difficult task for instructors. One semester might appear to have too little time to both hone one's critical awareness and make strides toward active problem-solving, and some modes of activism, like boycotts, protests, and community organizing, are not only impractical but also outside the scope of the instructor's duties.

Student activism in the twenty-first century, however, does not necessarily look the same as the activism of the 1960s. Given its influence and visibility, social media—rather than physical protests and rallies organized through various platforms—has become a primary site of activism today. As such, it might be useful to introduce to the curriculum some of the ways in which student protest via social media has inspired sociopolitical activism nationally and internationally. Depending on the school environment and the goals of the individual class, of course, the racial literacy curriculum may incorporate a community service module of some sort to turn in-class antiracist discourse into antiracist activism outside of the classroom. (Chapter 8 addresses this and other ways to bridge the classroom and the community.)

Instructors must also remind themselves of and express to their students that discourse itself, and particularly the reframing of problematic discourses, *can* effect change. If language has the power to oppress, then it also has the power to liberate. In conversation and writing, students can suggest and debate steps that might be taken on both individual and societal scales to combat racism.

Interrogating Race as a Discursive System

> "If I'm writing an essay, I want to send a message. I want to make you really interested. I want to twist it all in a way that you could see my point. And it's what they do on the news."
>
> —Amina (Arabic)

Scholars have suggested that educators and administrators "typically worry about racial inequality rather than the very idea of racial classification."[10] Because the avoidance of racial markers simply hides the ways in which racial inequities manifest themselves in the classroom, conversations about race must be framed with "honest, critically conscious discussion of *race talk itself and its dilemmas.*"[11] To begin to reconfigure the ways educators approach race inside and outside of the classroom "requires theorizing and teaching about race as a discursive system, not as individual words people use or as individual attitudes or behaviors."[12] In other words, it is important to consider how language both reflects and helps to construct ideologies about race, racialization, and racism. It is also important to consider how individuals approach conversations about race—after all, how can we encourage race talk and examine its significance if we haven't yet identified the discursive approaches individuals take to engage in such conversations?

Four primary modes have emerged in racial literacy scholarship to characterize students' approaches to race talk in the writing classroom: sharing, labeling, confronting stereotypes, and hedging. Table 1.2 summarizes the definition and function of each of these speech acts as well as its application in the composition classroom. To build a strong bridge to the goals of the critical writing classroom, exploring racial literacy as a paradigm for rhetorical analysis involves determining how the discursive practices of racial literacy lend themselves to the development of rhetorical skills integral to critical writing, including the establishment of authorial positionality and ethos in research and composition; critical readings of texts; drawing conclusions from data; attention to style, diction, and delivery; and awareness of audience.

CONCLUDING THOUGHTS

All individuals, regardless of their experiences or cultural identifications, are raced by virtue of living and attending school in a society in which skin color directly or indirectly influences not only their self- and social identities and day-to-day interactions with others but also their access to housing, health care, and indeed education. As such, all students and educators have the potential—and, some might say, the imperative—to practice racial literacy.

NOTES

1. Mara Lee Grayson, "Race Talk in the Composition Classroom: Narrative Song Lyrics as Texts for Racial Literacy," *Teaching English in the Two-Year College* 45, no. 2 (2017).
2. Suzanne de Castell and Allan Luke, "Defining 'Literacy' in North American Schools: Social and Historical Conditions," *Journal of Curriculum Studies* 15, no. 4 (1983): 380.
3. Conference on College Composition and Communication, "Students' Right to Their Own Language," *College Composition and Communication* (1974): 25.
4. For a discussion of the limitations of multicultural education, see Sonia M. Nieto, "Profoundly Multicultural Questions," *Equity and Opportunity* 60, no. 4 (2003): 6–10.
5. For more on culturally relevant pedagogy, see Gloria Ladson-Billings, "But That's Just Good Teaching! The Case for Culturally Relevant Pedagogy," *Theory into Practice* 34, no. 3 (1995): 159–65.
6. France Winddance Twine, "A White Side of Black Britain: The Concept of Racial Literacy," *Ethnic and Racial Studies* 27, no. 6 (2004): 878.
7. Lani Guinier, "From Racial Liberalism to Racial Literacy: *Brown v. Board of Education* and the Interest-Divergence Dilemma," *Journal of American History* 91, no. 1 (2004): 115.
8. Ibid.
9. Kristen A. Renn, "Creating and Re-Creating Race: The Emergence of Racial Identity as a Critical Element in Psychological, Sociological, and Ecological Perspectives on Human Development," in *New Perspectives on Racial Identity Development: Integrating Emerging Frameworks*, eds. Charmaine L. Wijeyesinghe and B. W. Jackson III (New York: New York University Press, 2012), 17.

10. Mica Pollock, *Colormute: Race Talk Dilemmas in an American School* (Princeton: Princeton University Press, 2004), 13.

11. Ibid., 218.

12. Michelle T. Johnson, "Race(ing) Around in Rhetoric and Composition Circles: Racial Literacy as the Way Out" (PhD diss., University of North Carolina, Greensboro, 2009), 160.

2

Prepare, Plan, and Provide

Developing Curricula within the Racial Literacy Framework

"Teachers who have been successful in promoting such dialogue consistently set up a class tone and structure that builds trust, normalizes conversations about race, and challenges assumptions about race and racism. . . . Such conversations require consistent and continuous practice, specifically when it comes to fostering dialogue at a deeper level."

—Amy Vetter and Holly Hungerford-Kressor[1]

An experienced hiker who sets off to guide a group of backpackers through a difficult trail must fill her knapsack with camping gear, extra clothing, ample foodstuffs, bug repellent, and all other provisions her clients require to endure the journey. She must show the rest of the group the paths available and walk ahead when necessary. But the experienced hiker must herself make the journey, traversing rough terrain, shielding from the elements, and stopping on occasion to marvel at the paradoxically infinite ephemera of nature. While this chapter addresses some considerations for instructors planning to teach racial literacy, it is important that this question be posed: Can racial literacy be taught?

Racial literacy is a continual process of learning with no definitive point of mastery. It is the active, continual observing, interpreting, questioning, and communicating necessary to understand race, racism, and antiracism. Like the backpacking guide, the racial literacy instructor must be willing to forego the role of the expert and remain instead a continuous learner. In the racial literacy classroom, teachers are not lecturers; they are well-prepared guides on their students' journey of racial literacy.

PART 1: PREPARATION

Researchers in teacher education classrooms have emphasized the need for preservice and in-service schoolteachers to develop racial literacy in order to better reach the students in their classrooms. This is an important field of inquiry and represents a key starting point for the development of racially cognizant pedagogies in secondary and postsecondary classrooms. Nonetheless, it is a big leap from racial literacy in teacher education to racial literacy in teachers' classrooms. Understanding racial literacy as a framework for equitable education does not guarantee success in implementing racial literacy *curricula* in English and composition classrooms.

Even teachers who understand or are interested in interrogating the functions of race in American society may not be wholly comfortable facilitating race talk in their own classrooms. As such, teachers must develop their own set of tools with which to interpret and discuss race to ensure that they neither silence race talk nor unintentionally reify racial inequity (see box 2.1).

The Instructor's Positionality

> "And I had always been a black woman instructor before. Which is why it was such a shock to meet the heat of a small group of students who became angry during a discussion initiated after another student's presentation on people of color in newsrooms nationally. What they said was, 'Why do we always have to talk about this?' This meaning the legacy of ongoing racism in American life? This meaning something that they did not want to talk about? This meaning topics in mass communications? . . . Very simply, the reason why I became an institutional target for moderating a discussion on structural racism and representation in a mass communications class was that I was a black woman faculty member who dared to demand that I be treated the same way as any other (read: white) faculty member."
>
> —Shannon Gibney[2]

Kimberley, a White racial literacy educator in the English department at a predominantly White university, was asked by the director of the Multicultural Affairs Center to appear on an interdisciplinary faculty panel addressing racism on campus. The panel, cosponsored by the Black Student Union, featured two other speakers: a Black sociologist and a Latina political scientist, both of whom had previously appeared on university panels. Later that week, Kimberley and her colleagues met over lunch to share ideas for the panel.

Maria, the political scientist, advised Kimberley, "The students who attend these talks are smart—and they're critical. They're going to ask what your role is here. Be prepared to address your privilege."

"I figured as much," Kimberley said. "When I started teaching here, I expected some resistance to my approach, but nobody's really said anything."

"Of course they haven't," said Carl, the sociologist. "You're White."

BOX 2.1. DEVELOPING A RACIAL LITERACY PRACTICE TO BECOME A RACIAL LITERACY EDUCATOR

Read. Familiarize yourself with the history and development of the racial literacy framework, studies into racial literacy development in the classroom, and the racial literacy framework as a paradigm for writing instruction. (For reading suggestions, check out the resource list at the end of this book.) Take note of what has worked in the past, and consider how those approaches might play out in your own classroom. Also pay attention to anything that frustrates, confuses, or intrigues you. Jot down those things, and hold them with you as you continue your racial literacy journey.

Write. Try out for yourself the writing activities suggested in this book. Draft your own "Racial Literacy Autobiography" and fill out your own "Positionality Cluster Map" (chapter 6); spend a week "Breathing to Write" at least once a day (chapter 5). Get to know your own history with race and racism. Interrogate the ways you see and are seen in the world. You may have written about this before, but do it again—and then again. Don't throw away any of these informal writings, even if you don't like what you've written; you may want to come back to them later on.

Reflect. Consider how you became interested in learning about the racial literacy framework and why you want to be a racial literacy educator. What do you bring to the classroom? What do you want to provide for your students? What do you still need to learn? Don't settle for easy answers—and don't expect that every question will have an answer. Go back to anything in your reading that stood out to you. After some time has passed since you began using the racial literacy framework—a few weeks, a few months, a year, or five—go back to your writing, and see if anything has changed about the ways you approach the activities.

Share. Talk to others. Explain to people you trust what you are working on and why it is important to you. Be open to their opinions and insights, even if their work is unrelated to your own. The scholarly perspective is only one of many, and it is important to understand how people outside of the academy conceive of race, racism, individual identity, and social positionality. Talk to people who are similar to you and those you know to have different cultural backgrounds. Ask relevant but respectful questions; recognize that those close to you may not be in the same place you are. If anyone seems to be resistant to discussion, gently inquire as to why—but don't push. Return to the conversation later if you have the opportunity. Everyone's racial literacy journey is unique, and right now, this is yours.

Like any writer or speaker, the racial literacy instructor must consider the ethos that he or she brings to the classroom. One difficult yet key part of preparation involves anticipating how students in the racial literacy classroom will respond to the instructor—based, at least in part, on his or her racial positionality.

Instructors of color doing this work may encounter resistance from White students—and colleagues—who accuse them of "having an agenda," "rocking the boat," or "playing the race card." Such responses mirror the institutional racism many instructors experience on a regular basis. Despite an increasingly diverse student population, instructors of color still make up an inordinately small percentage of university faculty. Moreover, the hiring of faculty of color does not guarantee that institutional norms will become more equitable.

Often, in fact, issues of racism are swept under the rug following these new hires and replaced with claims that the increased faculty diversity is evidence of postracialism. Sometimes, new faculty of color are assigned "diversity" courses, regardless of whether they have requested those courses or not, and genuine efforts toward structural equity may be discarded in favor of broad curricula that only scratch the surface of how race and racism play out on campus.

In the classroom, instructors of color who directly challenge White privilege and structural racism are at risk, paradoxically, of being accused of racism themselves. In the first story quoted in this chapter, for example, a Black woman professor at a predominantly White college received first complaints from students and then official sanctions from school administration for critiquing the inherent White privilege of news organizations. Unfortunately, situations like this are both why racial literacy curricula are needed and why they are difficult to implement.

Instructors who attempt to appease White students by avoiding direct discussion of structural inequity will both deprive students of an integral part of racial literacy education and find themselves feeling resentment and frustration that they are not teaching the curriculum racial injustice demands. On the other hand, deliberately bucking the system and bringing to the forefront structural inequity can alienate students (despite how problematic such a reaction is) and even jeopardize an instructor's job. There is no perfect way for an educator of color to address his or her own positionality in the classroom. The appropriate approach depends on many factors, including the student population, official course goals, and the amount of departmental and institutional support the instructor receives.

Due to the racism and privilege that prevail in educational institutions, White teachers will likely face fewer obstacles than their colleagues of color as they introduce racial literacy curricula. However, the White teacher whose race and privilege allow her to design a racial literacy curriculum without rebuke from administration or White students may encounter resistance in the classroom from students of color. Students may doubt the authenticity of a racial literacy curriculum led by a White instructor or even consider it an act of cultural appropriation. What right, some might wonder, does a White instructor have to talk about racism?

While it is true that Whites are not the victims of structural racism, their identification as White plays a role in maintaining racism. White instructors, therefore, can focus on what they *do* know not only as scholars but also as racialized individuals. Some antiracist educators have found that, when White teachers share their own experiences with race and racialization, students feel more comfortable sharing as well. During these discussions, Whiteness as a critical topic is made "more visible, less neutral."[3]

Racial literacy instructors must prepare to be questioned. They must be willing to subject their own positionality and privilege to scrutiny, even in the classroom. Most importantly, instructors seeking to implement a racial literacy curriculum must navigate the murky waters of their own positionality prior to establishing any curriculum that deals with matters of race or asks students to consider their roles as racialized beings within American society. Such a reflective process serves not only to make visible the biases that might influence an educator's instruction but also to acclimatize even the most experienced teachers to the challenges posed by race talk.

PART 2: PLANNING

Like all faculty, instructors who commit to teaching racial literacy are limited by time, departmental requirements, and resources. There is only so much that can be done in an academic year, let alone one semester, and the racial literacy curriculum is often only one component of many that instructors must take into account as they plan and teach their classes. These confines, along with the type of institution, its population of students, and its surrounding environment, all influence the concept and design of a racial literacy curriculum.

Institutional Considerations

A racial literacy educator must know his or her students before anyone enters the classroom. No, this doesn't mean an instructor should read course rosters before the semester begins and friend on social media all the students enrolled in his classes. He should, however, develop a sense of the institutional culture, the student population, and the surrounding community. Racial literacy instruction in a predominantly White classroom necessarily requires a different approach than instruction in a mostly Black classroom or a racially diverse setting. Racial literacy instruction also differs depending on the type of institution (private or public, two-year or four-year) and departmental requirements.

The Students

Teaching in a racially homogeneous classroom differs from teaching in a racially diverse classroom, but each setting comes with challenges and rewards for racial literacy instructors and students. In a racially homogeneous setting, it may initially seem easier for students to find common ground, which can help to create the sense of community the curriculum requires. Students with similar backgrounds may share similar experiences, language practices, and cultural reference points that make communication easier. Instructors may be pleased at first with how easily conversation flows.

However, the racially homogeneous classroom can make people seem deceptively similar, and the feeling of community that comes from frequent sharing and agreeing can actually distract from some of the deeper work of the racial literacy curriculum. When students share similar backgrounds and experiences, the deeper work must involve interrogating the conditions that have led to those similarities; identifying the differences between people who share a racial identification; and exploring, through texts or out-of-classroom communication, how their own experiences differ from the experiences of people of different races.

In a racially diverse setting, students may already have practice communicating across racial and cultural lines. Being surrounded by diverse peers can mislead students to believe they have more critical racial awareness than they actually do. Interacting with people of different races does not, by itself, confer an understanding of how race and racism factor into the lived experiences of individuals and groups in a society. Moreover, students may be deceived by the seeming ease with which people of different races interact, a misperception that can lead them to see race as less significant than it is in maintaining societal inequity. In the most diverse of classrooms, emphasis must be placed on ensuring all voices are heard.

In diverse classrooms, some students' voices may be inadvertently marginalized, especially if the curriculum erroneously addresses race in binary terms. Many students who do not identify as White or Black already feel left out of race talk. Exploring the limitations of how race is conceptualized is especially important in classrooms with large populations of students from marginalized groups that have been traditionally excluded from racial discourse.

The Location

Geography is key to understanding the functions of race, racialization, and racism, yet culturally relevant pedagogy and critical literacy studies are generally—though not exclusively—aimed at urban communities. There is logic to this, of course: Urban areas tend to be more racially, ethnically, linguistically, and socioeconomically diverse, necessitating increased awareness of how this diversity influences students' experiences, opportunities, social interaction, and frames of knowledge. Major metropolitan areas like New York City have long been key sites for planting the seeds of political revolution and social change.

At some point, however, these pedagogies must be taken outside urban centers and tailored to meet the needs of students in other communities. People in suburban and rural areas are not exempt from the forces of racism and essentialism and have the same need to interrogate and reflect on how their own beliefs and experiences have been shaped by those forces.

For example, mainstream representations of rural communities—"stories of rural backwardness or tales of an idealized past that never really was"[4]—do not represent the more complex narratives and experiences of those who live, teach, and learn in rural communities. Representations of rural Americans as ignorant and backward may not immediately appear to be racial stereotypes (because they do not fit our general conception of racism as existing within a White/non-White binary), but racial literacy curricula in rural environs must address the interplay here between race and geography.

Terms like *redneck*, *hick*, and *White trash* allow middle-class and wealthy White people to assert their racial and socioeconomic agency by categorizing the lives and behaviors of poor Whites as unexpected of or unacceptable for White people—effectively labeling poor Whites as distinctly *not* White. In doing so, they displace racism onto poor, rural, southern, and less-educated Whites while simultaneously reifying racist ideologies of essential distinctions between Whites and Blacks. Developing the rhetorical skills to talk back to this representation is necessary for students in rural communities as well as those in suburban and urban environments.

Suburbs are predominantly wealthier, Whiter, and less diverse than cities, and suburban schools by and large outperform schools in both urban and rural communities. Students in suburbs benefit from racial literacy curricula as well, though their needs may differ from the needs of students in rural areas or cities. That students in these schools are well served by the existing racial structures of society does not negate their need to interrogate the nature of those privileges. Those who profit from inequality rarely see those benefits, normalized and seemingly ordinary as they are. In order to disrupt inequitable racial hierarchies, however, White students must question White privilege, wealthy students must critique the distribution of wealth, and all students must come to understand how their own positions in society are maintained—for better or worse—by the existence of race, racialism, and racism.

The School

Sadly, many instructors do not receive institutional support to develop antiracist curricula. In some cases, ideological conflicts and institutional avoidance of anything deemed too political can prevent educators from creating and teaching explicit racial literacy courses. University administrators may see the curriculum as controversial and fear the repercussions of its implementation—and, one may argue, for good reason. Some of the standard practices of antiracist and social justice education, such as the critique of individual situations as microcosms of larger injustices or youth-led participatory action research (Y-PAR) projects that encourage students to examine the culture of their own schools and communities, can lead to public scrutiny around institutional norms.

Private schools, reliant on tuition and donor support, might be concerned about continuing enrollment or fear that wealthy donors will shy away from providing financial support for curricula that, in part, challenge the privilege of the wealthy class. Public schools, which tend to have fewer resources for new curricula, may hesitate to allocate needed funds to a program that isn't yet built into the core curriculum.

Recent discussion around trigger warnings and safe spaces in academia may also make officials wary of how students will respond if the curriculum causes them emotional discomfort. As a result, some schools will support the design of a racial literacy course but will want to temper its content to ensure that students are not offended. While ensuring student safety is of utmost importance, sheltering adult students from possibly uncomfortable material deprives individuals from potentially transformative learning experiences. Moreover, such efforts are often made not to alleviate the discomfort of students of color (who are traditionally underrepresented in higher education, both in terms of enrollment and course content) but to ease the possible discomfort of White students who might be forced to address their own privilege in the academy.

Even when the institution supports the content of a racial literacy course, there may be some debate about who should be teaching such a course and in which department. English departments may see racial literacy as belonging to a discipline like sociology, while a sociology department may deem the literacy emphasis of the framework as belonging to the field of education. In these cases, it helps to see the lack of disciplinary ownership as an asset rather than a deficit. Interdisciplinary ventures can be a very good way for instructors interested in teaching racial literacy to convince their programs of the value of the curriculum.

Sometimes the resistance to a racial literacy course will be more practical than ideological. Student enrollment is necessary to ensure that a course will run, and many students, especially those who have already declared majors and minors, will be reluctant to enroll in an elective course that does not fulfill the requirements they need to graduate on time. For this reason, it is a good idea for racial literacy educators to consider how they might work their courses into either the broad curriculum or the major fields in which they teach. Given the emphasis in racial literacy on discursive practices, instructors might consider requesting their courses be designated as writing-intensive or as fulfilling one of the broad areas of knowledge students are required to complete.

Even when student interest is high and the department and institution are in favor of antiracist curricula, approving new courses can be an arduous process. Approval is often required by more than one governing body, and the process can take an entire academic year. Tenured faculty with good standing will likely have the most success with this process, and in some cases, only tenured professors are permitted to design courses. For many instructors, especially junior and non-tenure-track faculty, it will be nearly impossible to design a racial literacy course from scratch. In such cases, instructors will need to conceive of ways to incorporate their racial literacy curricula into existing courses.

Fitting the Curriculum to the Course

> Jim, a newly hired composition scholar teaching a racial literacy curriculum in a required first-year writing course, was asked by his supervisor to share with his colleagues the ways he introduced the concept of authorial positionality into his classroom. Most of his English department colleagues had backgrounds in literary studies and emphasized reading rather than writing in their classes, a trend the composition director found increasingly problematic. Before Jim's presentation, however, his supervisor gave him a warning.
>
> "Don't talk too much about the racial aspect of the curriculum," she said. "A lot of people will get so caught up in that they'll forget they're teaching a writing course."

While literature, used properly, can be an important contribution to the composition classroom, that so many composition courses are taught by literature scholars who lack the preparation or interest to isolate composition from its literary counterparts in the English department is a long-standing problem in the field of composition studies.[5] Literary texts can, however, be very useful in the racial literacy curriculum (a point that is further addressed in the next chapter), but Jim's experience brings up another important consideration: Introducing racial literacy into an existing course curriculum demands that racial literacy be woven as seamlessly into the course fabric as possible to ensure that students' racial literacy work complements and supports (rather than distracts from) the other educational goals of the course.

First-Year Composition

First-Year Composition (FYC) functions for many students not only as their introduction to academic writing but also as part of their introduction to the college experience. For this reason, it is a uniquely fitting venue for the development and implementation of critical pedagogies that address both the academic skills and lived experiences of new college writers.

The needs of first-year students are unique. First-year students are simultaneously hopeful and overwhelmed. They are new to college, and college is new to them. Many freshmen expect college to be very different from high school, an expectation that is accompanied both by excitement and fear. The racial literacy focus in FYC can seem at once fascinating and overwhelming. Some students will be excited about the opportunity to address what they see as "real-world" concerns inside the classroom, while others might struggle to see the English classroom as more than an essay workshop.

The racial literacy curriculum emphasizes experiential modes of learning and places curricular focus on the student as creator, interpreter, and communicator. The self-reflective portion of the racial literacy curriculum is uniquely suited to the FYC classroom. In order for an individual to comprehend and critique the larger structures of race and racism that undergird society, she must first consider her own relationship to race and racism. A student-responsive approach to composition instruction must also begin with the individual before moving outward to the universal.

In its official position statement on postsecondary writing instruction, the Conference on College Composition and Communication, the world's foremost professional organization dedicated to the teaching and research of composition, claims that sound writing instruction frames writing as a situated practice shaped by the communities and contexts in which it occurs.[6] In the FYC classroom, teachers and students alike must initially identify and validate the literacy practices with which students are already familiar. By making explicit the ways in which students use language in their daily lives, they are better able to see how these practices are influenced by the communities of which they are a part and the cultures with which they identify. This focus also helps students identify how writing differs between and among communities, cultures, and academic disciplines.

In a situation like the one Jim experienced, it would be useful for instructors to highlight the critical writing and discursive rather than the sociological elements of the racial literacy curriculum. It is not enough for instructors to talk about race or tell their students that is OK to talk about race—instructors must be explicit about *why* we talk about race in a composition classroom. By doing so, instructors not only share the logic behind the curriculum, possibly preventing critiques of the curriculum as tangential, but also introduce students to some of the scholarly debates that define the field of composition studies.

Advanced Writing Courses

Advanced writing courses come in all shapes, sizes, and specializations. By the time students are enrolled in advanced writing courses, they are likely already entrenched in their major fields of study, which provides a wonderful opportunity for a more in-depth use of the racial literacy framework.

Students majoring in English, creative writing, writing and rhetoric, or linguistics might be especially interested in courses that connect the use of language with a sociopolitical exploration of racial (in)equity. A course like Race and Rhetoric might seem an obvious venue, but even a more traditional writing or linguistics course can make space for racial literacy: In a History of the English Language class, for example, instructors can emphasize how the language has developed and changed as a result of migration, immigration (voluntary or forced, as in the slave trade), urbanization, and the global economy.

A literature course could use the racial literacy framework as a critical lens for textual analysis of literary works by notable authors. A creative writing instructor could highlight the personal and reflective elements of the racial literacy curriculum by turning assignments like the racial autobiography (see chapter 6) into a longer memoir or by inviting students to craft poems or short works of fiction that explore individual identity. In a creative nonfiction or journalism course, students might explore a recent event or contemporary societal phenomenon using racial literacy as a framework for analysis.

Discipline-based writing courses, including field-specific Writing in the Disciplines courses (e.g., Writing for Engineering) and broader survey courses (e.g., Professional or Technical Writing), are ideal sites for racial literacy education. Academic and professional disciplines have discursive patterns of behavior, language, and argumentation that represent ways of communicating and creating knowledge within those disciplines. A racial literacy curriculum in interdisciplinary instruction can make explicit the ways disciplinary ideologies stem from or speak to racial and societal systems of hierarchy.

Interdisciplinary Instruction

Interdisciplinary approaches to composition are increasingly common in colleges and universities, particularly for first-year students. Learning communities allow students to situate their understanding of composition across disciplines and within real-world contexts and provide greater overall curricular coherence. Racial literacy is ideal for interdisciplinary courses because, put simply, race does not exist on its own nor does it belong to any one discipline.

Interdisciplinary ventures between sociology or history and composition, for example, might seem like obvious sites for racial literacy curricula (which they are), but other combined courses could also benefit from these curricula. A racial literacy curriculum in a learning community that connects composition with physics could explore the scientific contributions of traditionally underrepresented groups, like the Black women who worked for NASA in the 1960s. In a combined marketing and writing class, students could examine how racial stereotypes are used in advertising. With two dedicated instructors, courses from even the most seemingly disparate fields can be tied together effectively to encourage an interdisciplinary exploration of racial literacy (see box 2.2).

STEP 3: PROVIDING

Drafting the curriculum on a syllabus is only a step toward the provision of a successful racial literacy class. Everything can change when teachers and students enter the classroom—and the instructor must be willing to continue to learn.

Get to Know the Students Better

Once the students are in the classroom, instructors of racial literacy curricula can assign writing exercises that help them to get to know students more individually. In the first few days of class, it might be useful to assign an informal essay that is intended to help teachers to get to know the students as writers and individuals. Sometimes this is a simple get-acquainted essay with few guidelines: Students can write whatever they would like their instructors to know about them in the form of an essay as they understand it.

BOX 2.2. "WHAT IF
I'M NOT TEACHING COMPOSITION?"

Racial literacy is relevant to all disciplines. So is critical writing. Outside of composition studies, research into racial literacy development in the classroom has emerged from the fields of education, history, legal studies, science, and mathematics. The language we use as scholars and teachers and the discursive practices we use to communicate with members of our disciplines are always worth examining, as are the ways in which those practices reify or resist systemic racial inequity.

As you read through this book, consider how the suggestions for critical reading, writing, and communicating might play out in your own classrooms. Feel free to modify activities to better connect with your own disciplines and the logistics that accompany your teaching. For example, if you teach in a biology laboratory instead of a classroom, consider not only the formal structure and language patterns of lab reports but also how each lab table is arranged and how lab partners are assigned. Consider what students might see, hear, and feel in the room, and reflect on what you experience as a member of your field and as an instructor. Be sure to check out the resource list at the end of this book for more reading on racial literacy across the curriculum.

Depending on the explicitness of the racial literacy curriculum, the assignment may instead be more of a racial autobiography (see chapter 6), in which students are directly asked to explore their experiences with race and racism. In predominantly White classrooms, this assignment may prove difficult for students who have yet to see themselves as raced beings; as such, it is important that the instructor who is unfamiliar with the student population (because, for example, he or she is new to the school or community) be prepared to tailor this informal assignment to the students in the classroom.

Racial literacy instructors should also provide opportunities for students to reach out to them outside of the classroom. It is important to remember how much instructors ask of these young people each semester. In some universities, full-time students enroll in five courses each semester, each of which requires classroom time; study time; and often lab hours, testing, or essay writing.

On top of their academic duties, many students participate in extracurricular clubs or hold internships related to their paths of study; many others work part or full time to fund their education. Add to all of this the demands of family, friends, and romantic relationships, and it is easy to see why students may become overwhelmed at any given time. In addition to these personal, professional, and academic obligations, the racial literacy curriculum asks students to engage emotionally and sociopolitically with complex, often unsettling questions of identity and inequity.

As such, it is important that the racial literacy teacher be available to speak with students via e-mail or during office hours. It might even be a good idea to dedicate one or two class sessions per semester to individual conferences to ensure that instructors can check in with all students, including those whose other obligations prevent them from attending official office hours. These conferences are very useful if they are scheduled before a paper is due to help students stay on the right track or after a paper has been returned to go over the work's strengths and weaknesses and to discuss any suggested revisions. These individual conferences provide the one-on-one attention that is hard to come by in large classes; show students that their instructor is accessible; and help instructors to get to know students a little better, not only as people, but also as writers and racial literacy students.

Challenge the Black/White Binary

While racial literacy has not always been about diversity (in some of its sociological origins, racial literacy was largely about Black identity and socialization), an expanded understanding of racialization necessitates that racial literacy curricula address the ways in which all people of color, as well as White people, are racialized by virtue of their existence within American society. Racism is a structural system of advantage based on essentialist racial classification. Because institutions routinize and maintain the existing racial order, systemic racism influences the lived experiences of *all* individuals, yet those experiences may differ dramatically as a result of how individuals and groups are racially identified.

Non-Black groups of color have been racialized and minoritized throughout American history. Adding to that complexity, many of those who today are racially labeled as White, such as Jewish, Italian, and Arab people, have been victims of racism. In order to critique Whiteness and the privilege it affords, it is necessary to examine the history of race and racism. This is especially important in addressing the racialized experiences of all students, particularly those whose voices are silenced by the Black/White binary of traditional racial discourse. It is imperative that our racial literacy curricula do not inadvertently marginalize Asian, Native American, and other non-Black students of color, thereby not only reifying that inequitable binary but also failing to provide equitable education to the students in the classroom.

Successful curricula for racial literacy must also be intersectional, considering the ways in which other variables, such as socioeconomic class, ethnicity, geography, religion, gender, and sexuality, function in tandem with race, both on the individual and systemic levels. Students should be encouraged to consider their own individual positionality and identities as well as the ways in which the aforementioned variables influence broader societal issues and ideologies. The focus should remain, however, on how those variables intersect with race and racism. Many argue, for example, that socioeconomic stratification is one of the root causes of American inequity, but "all forms of oppression are about the distribution of resources . . . that does not negate the reality and salience of racism and how it *deepens and intensifies* the inequitable distribution of resources."[7]

Provide Ample Opportunity for Written Reflection

In many English departments, participation, as most often defined by contributions to class discussion, is a requisite criterion for student assessment. However, many students find it difficult to participate vocally in the classroom, especially when course material may be seen as controversial. While negotiating this reluctance is part of the racial literacy curriculum, instructors should supplement in-class discussion with written modes of participation, including online discussion boards and informal writing assignments (shared virtually or in small groups), to better include students who are uncomfortable speaking in class for personal or cultural reasons.

Written reflection in racial literacy curricula does more than ensure that all voices are heard: It provides students the opportunity to listen to and reflect on their own voices as students, writers, and racialized individuals. Personal writing allows students to identify the biases they may unconsciously possess that influence what they assume to be true about the world. By making tangible on the page what may otherwise remain uninvestigated, students begin to explore the situatedness of their own identities. The recognition of that situatedness helps students identify not only the deeply situated roles of race and racism but also the construction of experience, narrative, and text.

Put another way, telling their own stories invites students to explore the craft of storytelling itself. Frequent writing allows students to try out a variety of modes of composition in a low-stakes setting. Through informal, ungraded writing assignments, they may begin to develop and recognize the specific moves they make as writers, address patterns of errors, and hone the compositional skills they already possess.

Make Room for Student Expertise

Student-centered instruction, rather than lecturing (which draws the class's focus to the instructor) or testing (which places subject matter in a depersonalized vacuum), is the heart of the racial literacy curriculum. Curricula that incorporate active problem-solving, group work, and self-reflection engage students in ways that texts and lectures may not. By working through problematic situations and feeling the emotions, negative or positive, that arise therefrom, students are better able to forge connections with curricular materials.

For students to address systemic racialization and racism, they must accept their own participation in this system. Students must understand their racialized selves rather than assuming an identity that exists outside of the process of racialization. As such, the provision of information alone will not cultivate racial literacy; students practicing racial literacy must develop an embodied understanding of their own selves as racialized beings.

Small group work, open class discussion, lead-discussant activities, and student presentations also provide students opportunities to steer the curriculum in directions they believe to be of value. By providing guidelines and options for group and individual work, instructors can give students both space to guide the day's lesson and boundaries to ensure the class stays on track. Moreover, because race talk practices shed light on students' existing views on race and indicate their developing racial literacy, when teachers step back and listen to the particular ways in which students engage in race talk, they can track students' progress over the course of the semester.

Some antiracist and multicultural educators advise facilitators of race talk *not* to remain silent as conversations grow heated; allowing students to dominate conversation can display an instructor's "behavioral and emotional passivity."[8] Used strategically, however, silence can be an effective pedagogical choice in the racial literacy classroom. Making room for student expertise may occasionally mean allowing students to take missteps and learn through the conflicts that arise. Because conversation lends itself to the development of racial literacy, which must be "achieved in moment-to-moment interactions,"[9] developing discursive practices with which to address race is a key step in developing racial literacy.

Rather than relinquishing authority entirely, instructors can enter the conversation and encourage students to reflect once debate has either died down or reached an impasse. Heated conversation should not be seen as a negative part of classroom interaction; in fact, heated debate may be an integral component of racial literacy. Part of the facilitator's job is to ensure that those debates are productive rather than paralyzing. In order to ensure the focus remains on student learning rather than the provision of "right answers" from teachers, many of the techniques in box 2.3, such as the use of questioning and repetition of student voices, are intended to draw the conversation back to student voices and students' experiences. The teacher, therefore, enters the conversation only when needed to strategically mediate conflicts that have arisen between students or to illuminate connections between seemingly disparate perspectives or elements of the curriculum.

Continue to Reflect, Revisit, and Revise

It is the nature of the profession that teachers are constantly learning. Some of this learning is formal (graduate school, a teaching practicum, professional and faculty development workshops, and attending conferences), but the majority of that learning happens informally through the daily practices of teaching, observing, and reflecting. Teachers who have reflected on their early years as instructors or looked back at syllabi of years past, perhaps in order to compile a portfolio or craft a statement of teaching philosophy, have likely experienced the feeling of amazement (or amusement?) that comes from the sudden recognition of just how insufficient those old materials now appear in more experienced eyes.

In professional development and continuing education and on their own, teachers must continue to reflect on and revise their own experiences as individuals and as instructors. As teachers practice racial literacy in their own lives and writing, they become better able to bring equitable racial literacy curricula to their students.

BOX 2.3.   THE TEACHER'S TOOLBOX
FOR FACILITATING IN-CLASS CONVERSATION

Ask Questions

Asking questions puts the focus on the students and allows them to explore in greater depth their own feelings and perspectives.

- Request clarification if you're not sure of the meaning of a student's statement.
- Ask for details or examples to help make tangible abstract concepts.
- Gently probe when a student seems unsure of his or her own thoughts or feelings. The ideas might be there, even if a student is having trouble articulating them.
- If a student is resistant, *ask* if he or she would like time to think more before sharing.

Repeat Student Comments

Repeating or rephrasing what students have said shows that you're listening and that you value their contributions. Try some of the following:

- "I hear you saying . . ."
- "I'm thinking of that comment you made regarding . . ."
- "That reminds me of what _____ said about . . ."

Make Connections to Course Material

Regardless of the emotional and interpersonal content of this curriculum, drawing the conversation back to the course content reminds students that there is important material to be learned and that their experiences and ideas are a valuable part of academic knowledge.

- Refer students to course texts that provide similar, contradictory, or illuminating perspectives.
- Ask students if the stories they or their peers have shared remind them of anything they've read in class.
- Connect their comments to larger theories and concepts discussed in the course.

Because the meaning and implications of race are constantly changing, racial literacy must continue to adapt as well. Teachers, therefore, must remain students, open to new language, ideas, and methods of instruction and inquiry.

No matter how well-planned, no racial literacy curriculum will be perfect or hassle-free, especially once teacher and students enter the classroom. Like all good teachers, racial literacy instructors must frequently reflect on their own teaching; revise their methods to best meet the needs of their students; and stay up to date on current scholarship as well as the social, cultural, and political conditions that continue to necessitate racial literacy curricula. The instructor's continual engagement with racial literacy as a pedagogical framework and a scholarly field of inquiry may not prevent all problems that arise, but it will provide teachers with the tools necessary to work through, rather than around, those difficulties.

CONCLUDING THOUGHTS

Without careful planning, the racial literacy curriculum can become unfocused, uncomfortable, or tangential to other course material. Even the most carefully planned curricula can present problems, from in-class tensions between students to departmental or institutional resistance to course content. By taking time in advance to prepare to teach racial literacy; plan an equitable, relevant curriculum; and provide the tools necessary for students to feel safe and supported in the classroom, teachers may anticipate and prevent problems that could arise.

The racial literacy curriculum should be student-responsive and logically scaffolded, and both the overarching trajectory and individual assignments should tie in clearly to course goals. Because the racial literacy curriculum depends on student participation and self-reflection, assignments that are too abstract, too broad, or too specific with regards to personal information are likely to be alienating and ineffective. Instructors should consider carefully the assignments they choose and, to ensure that they are not demanding more than they themselves would give, should practice on their own every assignment they consider assigning the students in their classrooms.

Racial literacy is a continual practice of critical learning with no definitive end point. As such, a racial literacy teacher is always a racial literacy student. It is important, too, that instructors emphasize this perspective to their students: There is no perfection to be sought through racial literacy. Over the course of a semester or academic year, students may take small steps or giant leaps, and each student will begin from her own starting point. There is no specific finishing line. Work in the racial literacy classroom involves the development and refinement of the critical skills needed to talk back to injustice—and this process continues, for teachers and students, even after coursework has ended. The next few chapters explore some pedagogical approaches that may encourage this continual engagement, both inside the classroom and beyond its walls.

NOTES

1. Amy Vetter and Holly Hungerford-Kressor, "'We Gotta Change First': Racial Literacy in a High School English Classroom," *Journal of Language and Literacy Education* 10, no. 1 (2014): 83.

2. Taiyon J. Coleman, Renee DeLong, Kathleen Sheerin DeVore, Shannon Gibney, and Michael C. Kuhne, "The Risky Business of Engaging Racial Equity in Writing Instruction: A Tragedy in Five Acts," *Teaching English in the Two-Year College* 43, no. 4 (2016): 360.

3. Carlin Borsheim-Black, "'It's Pretty Much White': Challenges and Opportunities of an Antiracist Approach to Literature Instruction in a Multilayered White Context," *Research in the Teaching of English* 49, no. 4 (2015): 416.

4. Mara C. Teiken, *Why Rural Schools Matter* (Chapel Hill: University of North Carolina Press, 2014), 117.

5. See Maxine Hairston, "The Winds of Change: Thomas Kuhn and the Revolution in the Teaching of Writing," *College Composition and Communication* 33, no. 1 (February 1982): 76–88; and Erika Lindemann, "Freshman Composition: No Place for Literature," *College English* 55, no. 3 (1993): 311–16.

6. Conference on College Composition and Communication, *Principles for the Postsecondary Teaching of Writing*, revised March 2015, http://www.ncte.org/cccc/resources/positions/postsecondarywriting.

7. Robin DiAngelo, *What Does It Mean to Be White? Developing White Racial Literacy* (New York: Peter Lang, 2016), 270.

8. Derald Wing Sue, *Race Talk and the Conspiracy of Silence: Understanding and Facilitating Difficult Dialogues on Race* (Hoboken, NJ: Wiley, 2015), 231.

9. Rebecca Rogers and Melissa Mosley, "A Critical Discourse Analysis of Racial Literacy in Teacher Education," *Linguistics and Education: An International Research Journal* 19, no. 2 (2008): 125.

3

Reading, Writing, and Multimodality

Text Selection in the Racial Literacy Curriculum

"The brain, it seems, does not make much of a distinction between reading about an experience and encountering it in real life; in each case, the same neurological regions are stimulated."

—Annie Murphy Paul[1]

For years, English education scholars have debated which texts are most suited to the teaching and learning of literacy skills, including critical reading and writing. Some have argued, in fact, that what students read is not as important as how they read it.[2] Both are important in the racial literacy classroom, and instructors must be deliberate in their consideration of the texts they introduce into the curriculum. Different texts encourage students to read differently, think differently, and write differently.

READING IN THE RACIAL LITERACY CLASSROOM

A multimodal approach to text selection can both challenge students' critical literacy skills in a variety of ways and demonstrate for students the myriad modes of expression available to them as critical writing students (see box 3.1). In addition to more traditional classroom texts, like short stories, poems, scholarly essays, and news articles, instructors should also consider song lyrics, films, television episodes, YouTube videos, tweets, and other digital and social media.

In the racial literacy classroom, reading response assignments and exploratory essays encourages students to consider the ways race and related factors might influence a text's construction and meaning, as well as their own interpretations thereof. While this lens bears some similarities to a cultural studies perspective of literary criticism, the emphasis of this curriculum is not literary criticism per se but the craft

BOX 3.1. MULTIMODALITY

An approach of **multimodality** recognizes that multiple modes, styles, and practices are used to communicate meaning and acknowledges that communication is more than solely linguistic. While print texts have long been the mainstay of classroom instruction, visual, digital, and aural modes of communication are increasingly prevalent in contemporary life and, therefore, demand students to develop proficiency in interpreting and responding to these various texts. A theory of multimodality assumes that all texts—even traditional print-based texts—employ more than one mode of communication. In the classroom, this means that students must learn how different modes of communication work, for which reasons, and in which contexts. More practically, a multimodal approach to text selection in racial literacy involves acknowledging the multiple literacies in which students need to become proficient by incorporating print texts, media, and digital modes of communication—and those that are composed of more than one mode. Just as importantly, students must learn to compose their own texts with the concept of multimodality in mind.

of critical writing. Reading various texts serves both to illuminate underlying racial and sociocultural ideologies and to make explicit for students the constructedness of ideology through composition. In other words, students learn not only what texts say (in text and subtext) but also how those meanings and ideas are constructed through language.

RACIAL LITERACY TEXTS

Like everything else in the racial literacy classroom, there is no single text that is the best practice for teaching racial literacy. Instructors should choose the texts and types of texts that best fit their understanding of the curriculum, students' needs, and overall course goals. Broadly, texts should address—directly or obliquely—the following personal and structural components of race and racism (among others): institutional racism; racial identity development; White privilege; the role of language in race, racism, and racialism; the political use of race in the public sphere; the constructedness of race; and the intersections between race and other demographic variables. The curriculum should include both texts that help students understand the racial literacy framework and texts that encourage them to employ the framework.

The following are a sampling of the types of texts that might be helpful to include when teaching racial literacy and critical writing. (Specific titles that have been shown to be useful in teaching racial literacy can be found in the reference list at the end of this book.)

Nonfiction

While racial literacy learning moves beyond the provision of information to address emotion and unconscious bias, sometimes students need data to concretize racism, which can seem broad and abstract to those who have yet to analyze how it plays out in their own lives. For starters, students need to read texts that identify and define the basic concepts of the course, from the racial literacy framework to relevant terminology, like *race*, *racism*, and *racialization*. Establishing a common language in the classroom early on facilitates smoother discourse and prevents semantic misunderstandings.

Eventually, instructors can introduce texts that define terms and concepts differently. These texts can allow students to see how concepts are defined differently in different academic disciplines, within different sociopolitical arenas, or by different individuals and how academic and social understandings of race have changed over time.

Research results, such as statistics on societal problems like poverty, education, and the prison industrial complex, may make evident the extreme racial biases in long-standing social and governmental institutions. Data can initially be addressed briefly with the goal of gathering information, but later, once students have expanded their racial literacy skill sets, the same data should be examined more thoroughly to explore how such information is collected, analyzed, interpreted, and distributed. Reading nonfiction documents like research articles, journalistic essays, and investigative reports encourages students to more critically explore the themes of the course and to examine the craft and rhetoric of writing academic essays and research reports.

The racial literacy framework holds that systemic racism is apparent in individual situations. Nonfiction texts, such as memoirs and personal essays, provide so-called "real-life" accounts of individuals' experiences with racism, which can help make larger issues of inequity tangible and demonstrate for students less-visible aspects like emotion. For some students, these texts will serve as validation: Seeing in print situations similar to those they have experienced makes individuals feel less alone. In particular, these texts may make students of color, whose stories are too often underrepresented in the academic canon, feel welcome in the classroom.

Some students will be relieved to hear their voices in these texts and hope that, through these readings, their peers will understand them better; others, especially those who have encountered similar texts in previous classrooms, may be more skeptical that their peers will truly understand them. Familiar stories will likely evoke strong emotional responses, negative or positive, and can be a good starting point to a discussion of equity and representation in educational spaces.

Memoirs of racial literacy and antiracist activism show students that the racial literacy journey is real. Because stories of coming to racial literacy, antiracism, or White alliance are often nonlinear and filled with as many stumbling blocks as successes, these texts can provide a great deal of comfort and grounding for students who are struggling with some part of their own racial literacy journeys. Additionally, reading personal essays and memoirs in the racial literacy classroom may help prepare students to craft their own personal writings, an activity that is integral to the practice of critical writing in racial literacy (see chapter 6).

Fiction

> "I keep thinking about how little information there is about the wife in the story. We don't even know her name. I've been trying to write about the role of women in the story and I have to keep asking myself what isn't in the text."
>
> —Brenda (Ecuadorian)

While many university writing programs have moved away from teaching literature in First-Year Composition (FYC), many English departments still use literary texts as the primary reading material in writing classes. Whether this is appropriate is outside the scope of this book, but in the racial literacy classroom, fiction texts can be a useful addition to the curriculum. Reading fiction may engage students on a more personal level than could be achieved solely through the examination and practice of written academic discourse. As literature deals with narrative and human experience, it offers students the potential to grow as individuals and members of a community rather than only as scholars.

Through the taking on of another's perspective, individuals begin to examine their own interpretations and assumptions. Adult educational theories of transformative learning suggest that trying to see the world through another perspective allows room for the shift of one's own viewpoint and is essential for the achievement of transformation.[3] It is reasonable to argue, then, that as it is often through fiction that students are given access to other worlds and other experiences, including those significant to cultures dissimilar to their own, the reading of fiction provides a method through which students in the racial literacy classroom might work toward transformative learning. It is here that narrative's implications for the development of racial literacy begin to emerge.

Some of the qualities of fiction that make it suitable for the racial literacy curriculum are similar to those of memoir and personal essay. However, in fiction, questions of characterization and representation become even more significant. Because a reader has no assumption that the material presented in a story is true (as is the case with memoir), there is no implicit trust in the narrative voice. Fictional stories explore not only what has happened but what *could* happen (or could have happened), thereby providing readers opportunities to imagine; through fiction, racial literacy students can explore worlds different from those they know and consider how those worlds may come to be. Historical fiction, for example, may be useful in helping students gain a more emotional, insider experience of past manifestations of racism.

Reading fiction also enables students to consider how authors characterize individuals with regards to race, as well as other demographic identifiers, like ethnicity, gender, religion, and socioeconomic class. Studying individual characters can help students to see how texts may racialize and represent even fictional people. How are people of different races depicted? Who is present in the text? Who is absent?

Texts about Race

In the racial literacy classroom, reading texts that directly address race and racism makes it clear that these are the central foci of the course. This prevents students from steering conversation away from matters of race, as many individuals do to avoid the discomfort or sense of personal responsibility that accompanies race talk.

Exploring *how* different types of texts address race is especially important. How does the novelist address race compared with the scholarly researcher? What is the songwriter's approach or the essayist's? What does one poet do that another does not? What might account for such differences? Once students begin to note the differences between texts, they can also consider how those differences—be they generational, geographic, cultural, or academic—influence an individual author's positionality and orientation to racial discourse.

Moreover, texts that directly discuss race may be quite complex, and in the racial literacy classroom, it is possible to examine how a single text may address race in ways that are simultaneously equitable and problematic. For example, Harper Lee's *To Kill a Mockingbird*, which for many years has been required reading for high school students, was once heralded as an antiracist text (and arguably was indeed written as such) due to its critique of the unjust prosecution of a Black man in the Great Depression–era southern United States. However, some racially aware instructors today both address this aspect of the text and its depiction of the lawyer Atticus Finch as a White savior, a move that diminishes the agency of Tom Robinson, the Black defendant whose trial is central to the story. A full exploration of Lee's novel in the racial literacy classroom would both address the White-savior narrative it perpetuates and look to the novel's historical context to examine why that story would not have functioned without a White man advocating for Tom Robinson.

Texts Not about Race

Evelyn, a Puerto Rican woman studying a racial literacy curriculum in her freshman composition course, was assigned to read a personal essay for homework. The essay was about a woman's attempts to raise her children despite her husband's unemployment and alcoholism. The next time the class met, Evelyn immediately told her professor, "I looked up the author online, and she was a Hispanic woman. I didn't think she would be Hispanic when I read the story."

> Evelyn's professor asked her to share her observations with the rest of the class. While only a handful of the twenty-five students in the class identified as White, all but two students said that they, too, had assumed the author to be White.
>
> "I thought she was White," said Luther, a Black-identifying student. "I'm surprised everyone else thought so, too."
>
> "Why did you think she was White?" the professor asked.
>
> "Honestly? It wasn't the story. I just assume most stuff we read is by White people, especially in school."
>
> "Plus," said Evelyn, "I don't really think a Latina woman would have put up with it. I mean, no one in my family would. We expect men to provide for us."

While the racial literacy curriculum must incorporate material that brings to the forefront matters of race and racism, it is equally important for teachers to introduce texts that *don't* explicitly address race and racism. Some of the most productive conversations in the racial literacy curriculum may occur during the discussion of texts that seemingly have little to do with race. Racial ideology factors into even the most seemingly unrelated texts—as well as how students read them.

In the situation described here, Evelyn finds it difficult to imagine that a woman of an ethnic background similar to hers would tolerate a husband who fails to support his family. While she has drawn on her personal experiences as a self-identified Latina woman to support this assumption, she has also effectively essentialized all Latina women based on her observations of women she knows personally. Moreover, she uses the term *Latina*, which describes a woman of Latin American descent, interchangeably with the term *Hispanic*, a word that denotes a Spanish-speaking person or a person of similar ancestry. The instructor should note this usage and return to a discussion of the terms used for ethnic classification at another time.

Luther, on the other hand, seems to base his assumption about the author of the essay on his past experiences in academia. He is correct in his observation that most of the literature historically assigned in educational institutions has been written by White authors. In this situation, the instructor might ask Luther how he feels about this trend before opening up a larger conversation about representation in school curricula and its effects on students of color in the classroom. It is especially noteworthy that most of the students in the classroom assumed the author to be White. Once such a phenomenon is addressed, racial literacy educators can encourage students to interrogate their initial impressions and unconsciously held stereotypes about texts, their authorship, and their content.

Additionally, sometimes racism and racialization in texts are not obvious, especially during a first reading. Race is always salient, but it is not always visible. Racism, too, may be implicit rather than overt. In order for students to learn how to critically analyze the role of race in texts, they must read texts in which race does *not* take center stage—yet matters nonetheless. For example, rather than portraying complex personalities, characters may be depicted in ways that perpetuate racial stereotypes, or plots may reify rather than challenge existing racial hierarchies. Instructors in the racial literacy classroom can pose questions that expose the implicit racialization in a particular text.

Introducing texts that do not directly address themes of race and racism may be a useful strategy in engaging reluctant students in classroom activities. Despite the fact that the racial literacy curriculum is built on honest and direct discussion, straightforward texts can intimidate students and lead to evasive, indirect, or overly polite contributions to conversations—or, worse, silence. While such a reaction is problematic and worthy to address in the racial literacy classroom, teachers must choose their battles, and on occasion, it may be wise to allow race talk to emerge rather than demanding it. Once that race talk emerges and uneasy students begin to edge their way into the discussion, instructors may initiate a more direct critical discourse.

Nontraditional and Media Texts

"There's always been police brutality, right? But now it's shown on social media so much that it's making more people aware. And the news is broadcasting about it so much more, so maybe that's why there's so many people involved compared to before when, even if it happened all the time, it wasn't going on Facebook or Instagram."

—Tina (Dominican American)

Given the role media, including but not limited to television, film, music, and social media, play in students' lives, it is imperative that the racial literacy curriculum help students interrogate the ways in which media reinforce—and, at times, resist—existing hegemonic structures. There are five core tenets of what scholars have called *critical media literacy*:

1. *Nontransparency*, the understanding that all messages conveyed by media are constructed;
2. *Codes and Conventions*, the recognition of the language practices in media and the distinctions between the denotation of what we see from the connotation it bears;
3. *Audience Decoding*, that any media message can and will be received and interpreted differently by different audiences;
4. *Content and Message*, the embedded values and ideologies that have influenced the creation of a media text; and
5. *Motivation*, that all media are motivated by profit or power.[4]

Media messages are frequently naturalized and their constructedness rarely questioned. As such, to understand the concepts of critical media pedagogy, it is crucial that any media curriculum—including the racial literacy curriculum—introduce discursive practices for recognizing and questioning the ways they function in popular media and society.

The following are a few types of media that have proven particularly useful in engaging students in the practice of racial literacy.

Song Lyrics

Song lyrics incorporate simile, metaphor, meter, and often rhyme, among other formal elements that facilitate their easy comparison to more traditional print poetry. Other song lyrics follow conventions of narrative similar to those present in short stories. More important than their formal resemblance to more traditional classroom texts is this: While students often see literature as purely academic (whether that is actually the case or not), music is popular and accessible. Because of music's ubiquity in young people's lives—and because young people are often at the forefront of music and other pop culture trends—bringing music into the classroom puts students on a level playing field with one another and even the instructor.

Scholarship dating back to the 1960s has addressed the use of popular music to engage students in literary analysis. It may date back even further, actually—instructional practices of Progressive-Era literacy education introduced film and radio texts into the classroom, paving the way for contemporary education's more extensive pedagogical forays into music-based literacy instruction. A wealth of scholarship in the past two decades has attested to the unique power of hip-hop music and culture to teach composition and literary analysis, as well as to integrate marginalized students into classroom discussion. Originally addressed in secondary classrooms, hip-hop-influenced curricula are gradually making their way into college English courses, as well.

Some educators have found that incorporating socially and culturally relevant music into the most racially and ethnically diverse college classrooms helped form a sense of "kinship between students from various backgrounds."[5] This quality makes it especially useful in the racial literacy classroom. Using song lyrics as racial literacy texts invites students to explore how musicians of different genres address race and racism, as well as how particular genres speak to—or are marketed to—particular racial and cultural groups. The next chapter provides an extended example of a song-lyrics-based racial literacy curriculum.

Film

Karina began her writing classes every semester by assigning what she called an "informal getting-to-know-you essay." There were no guidelines for the assignment, and Karina didn't grade the papers. The only marginal comments she made were short notes meant to help her connect with her students and vice versa. Karina believed that students would feel more comfortable in the classroom if she talked to them on the page as a person rather than only their teacher.

One student, Shawna, opened her informal essay by writing that she always listened to music when she wrote: "Right now, I'm listening to Tupac." In purple pen in the margins, Karina wrote "Love Tupac!" When she returned the papers to the students, Shawna laughed and asked Karina what her favorite song was. At first, Karina felt Shawna was testing her, but as the conversation continued and as new conversations took place over the next few class sessions, Karina started to feel as though she'd earned her student's trust.

After the semester ended, a biopic of rapper Tupac Shakur opened in movie theaters. The next weekend, Karina received an e-mail from Shawna, her former student. Shawna had seen the Tupac biopic and, like most critics, hadn't been a big fan. Karina wrote, "They focused so much on how he was an activist as a rapper that they glossed over everything else, like gang violence and poverty and everything he rapped about. It was so one-dimensional! I've been wondering how we would have talked about it in class from the racial literacy perspective."

Film texts in the racial literacy classroom may include documentaries, features of any movie genre, or biopics of notable cultural and political figures. Students like Shawna can watch biopics and explore what they believe to be the central narrative and conflict: Is the movie an autobiography of sorts? If the protagonist is a musician, is the music the priority, or is the musician's personal life featured front and center? Films may help students to consider rhetorical elements like context, authorial choice, and audience. Showing recent films about racism, such as *Get Out*, *I Am Not Your Negro*, and *13th*, alongside older movies in which race plays a major role, like *Guess Who's Coming to Dinner*, can invite students to consider how race has been addressed rhetorically over time.

Film texts may enable students majoring in media studies, theater, and other visual arts to draw connections between their fields of study and the racial literacy curriculum. Perhaps most significant, however, is that, in part because film is visual, it has been shown to more fully engage the most reluctant writing and racial literacy students. Some racial literacy educators have found that dramatizing instances of racism affords students a more embodied, experiential understanding of race's role in society, historically and today.[6] This may be true even when students are not themselves the performers; the physicality of injustice as seen on film may concretize the effects of racism for students who have difficulty grasping—or who even deny—its persistence in contemporary society.

Additionally, students who have had negative experiences with literature and composition classes in the past may find film more accessible than traditional print texts. Instructors can in fact use film to explore the differences between *writing* and *composing* a text and may explain to students that a composition—even one that is primarily written, as is the case with academic essays—may indeed include other modes of communication, including graphics and digital media. As with any text used in a writing classroom, however, instructors should ensure that more important than the films themselves are what and how students write in response to them.

Advertisements

On the first day of the fall semester during which Rob, a racial literacy educator, began teaching a required Advanced Composition course in a university known primarily for its business school, a handful of students expressed concern that the curriculum might not be applicable to their fields of study. While Rob's first instinct was to say that race is always applicable, once he thought about it, he realized that perhaps the short stories and scholarly essays he'd listed on the syllabus were not the most useful texts for engaging the many finance and marketing majors in his classroom.

The next time the class met, Rob distributed a revised syllabus; he'd kept the scholarship but replaced the short story titles with a list of advertising campaigns. While some students remained hesitant, others grew more engaged as they began to scan the list of advertisements.

"What do you think?" Rob asked.

"I've seen this cereal commercial," a marketing major said. "We talked about it in my Consumer Behavior class."

"I took that class, too," said another student. "You know what? That commercial always did seem kinda racist."

Rob's story demonstrates three things: (1) the need for instructors to design their course curricula with the student population in mind, (2) the flexibility required of racial literacy educators, and (3) the potential usage of television and print advertisements in the racial literacy classroom.

While students today, like all of us, are inundated with advertisements, many of which are artistic ventures in their own right, like the stylized commercials that air during the Super Bowl, students do not always recognize that the primary motivation of this art is sales. In fact, the fields of marketing and advertising base much of what they show on psychological and sociological research. In order to sell items, ad campaigns sell ideas—and ideals.

Advertisements appeal to consumers by reflecting people's dreams and desires. It is common, for example, to display elements of the American dream, like the two-parent family of a mother and father, happy children, and lovable pets that run around the big, bright kitchen, making a mess that is easily cleanable with the right tile scrub. Whether individual consumers harbor these fantasies or not, ideals like the American dream are ingrained in the larger cultural ideology. As such, commercials and print advertisements tend to follow culturally normative patterns of behavior; they employ stereotypes because people recognize stereotypes.

On the other hand, because companies must appeal to the changing needs and ideas of the public, advertisements may in fact make strides toward equity in representation (regardless of their motivation). Those same companies that perpetuated stereotypes of mothers at home while fathers worked now show fathers doing laundry, gay couples feeding their children, interracial couples celebrating their engagement, and women frantically rushing to work in the morning.[7]

In the racial literacy classroom, advertisements invite students to critique not only how individual advertisements perpetuate or challenge stereotypes but also how the pervasiveness of marketing in our society contributes to our personal and cultural beliefs about race, gender, and sexuality.

Social Media

Ever-increasing participation in social media, particularly among young people, necessitates that racial literacy skills are fostered in students of all ages. Social media today represents a primary site of social engagement and political resistance. Sites like Twitter, Facebook, and Instagram have been useful in organizing protests; spreading awareness about boycotts; and designing online campaigns to raise funds for political movements, medical research, and even personal necessities.

Social media may also present obstacles to a full understanding of racism in society. Because much of what an individual user sees on Facebook or Instagram is based on insular social networks of friends and algorithms that take into account that individual's past Internet usage, users may only see one perspective on any given issue. Additionally, the proliferation of fake news from sensationalist websites makes it even more difficult for individuals to obtain accurate information and a full range of ideas about social and political issues.

Despite—or perhaps because of—these problems, social media texts have been shown to be uniquely useful in helping students to develop racial literacy. Social media venues already function as an outlet for individual citizens to share their views; on YouTube, for example, some users distribute directly or indirectly racist videos under the guise of free speech. Without the provision of formal concepts or language with which to discuss these videos, viewers may overlook the ways in which such videos not only reinforce stereotypes but also propagate the message that such views are acceptable in online forums. Scrolling through the comments section of some of these problematic videos shows that many commenters who resist the racism present in such videos themselves employ sexist and misogynistic language. Scholars have suggested that, in the racial literacy classroom, reading such comments could "facilitate discussion about how oppression can be reproduced even when resisting racism."[8]

INSTRUCTIONAL STRATEGY: STUDENT-SELECTED TEXTS

Returning to the example of Shawna, the student who wrote to her professor after seeing the Tupac Shakur biopic, it is clear that she felt the film, either because of or in spite of its flaws, would have been an important text to discuss in the racial literacy classroom. Unfortunately, in Shawna's case, the semester had already ended (though it is quite possible that Karina, her professor, will introduce the text in a future semester). Had the movie been released when class was still in session, it might have been possible for Karina, having heard Shawna's suggestion, to have assigned a viewing or even, depending on the institution and available funds, to arrange a class field trip to see the film.

Inviting students to bring their own texts into the classroom—and then incorporating those texts into the curriculum—encourages students to critically consider why certain texts appeal to them and demonstrates that their contributions are valued in the racial literacy classroom. In their other classes and their out-of-school lives, students are exposed to different texts than those their teachers and even their classmates encounter. Student input in text selection, therefore, increases the diversity of texts to which all students in the class are exposed.

On the individual level, when students select their own reading material, they are more likely to remain engaged in their reading. Equally significant is a student's reflection on why a particular text resonates with him or her. In this way, the student-selected text can be a jumping-off point for a personal essay. Student-selected texts can also serve as sources for analytical essays, informal reading commentaries, or in-class discussion.

A word of caution, however: When a student is familiar with a particular text, he may be more likely to stick to his initial impression or analysis and resist other students' contributions or alternate takes on the text. He may want to be seen as the expert on that text—and if that is the case, the instructor should let him. The feeling of agency can go a long way toward increasing a student's sense of himself as a scholar. At the same time, it is important that the instructor emphasize the reader's role in meaning making; different readers will have different experiences with any given text.

While the student who contributed that text to the curriculum should be allowed to briefly assume the role of expert, he should also support that stance with textual and extratextual evidence. For a student-selected text to be included in the classroom, the student must make some argument for its inclusion in the racial literacy curriculum. As such, when students contribute texts, they are also exercising their analytical and persuasive skills.

WRITING ABOUT RACIAL LITERACY TEXTS

In the racial literacy classroom, more significant than text selection is how students write in response to those texts. Writing assignments need not be directly related to the texts they have read; rather, those texts should inspire the writing students do in the classroom and at home. These assignments should not, however, resemble the book reports students might have written in high school or the literary criticism taught in the literature classroom. Instead, writing should provide an opportunity for students to connect to the texts they read, both personally and critically.

Teacher Resource: The Reading Commentary

English educator Sheridan Blau has suggested that "writing assignments into which students are unable to read themselves" disengage students and impede their growth as writers.[9] The commentary is a reading response of sorts in which students are invited to write their thoughts on, reactions to, and criticisms of assigned reading—prior to discussing the reading in the classroom. Writing the commentary before the in-class discussion not only gives students some material to contribute in the classroom, but it also allows them to express their ideas unclouded by the ideas of their peers or instructor.

The only requirement of a commentary is that it is a contribution to an academic discussion. Everything else is variable. In terms of length, the student should have room enough to explore his or her ideas, but it is unnecessary to go into so much depth that the commentary turns into an essay. This often amounts to somewhere between one and two pages, though it is advised that instructors do not assign page counts until they have seen what students produce without direction. Students should always know that the ideas they raise in their commentaries may be explored more fully in longer papers later in the semester. The content and approach to the commentary may also vary; students may write in the first person—or they may not. They may or may not refer to other texts. They may or may not connect the texts with their own personal experiences. The language, style, and form are all up to the students.

The first commentaries students write may begin with simple statements—even those that students may have been told in high school *not* to include in academic papers. "I like it," for example, is a fine starting point. "I like it" *is* a contribution and can lead to discussion of the role of opinionated statements in different genres of writing. Readers of movie reviews, for example, engage with those texts to see whether a trusted critic likes a film or does not. Students starting out this way might benefit from reading reviews that go beyond blanket statements of like or dislike and explain what has piqued their interest and why.

Reading the work of reviewers who are celebrated as writers, like film critic Roger Ebert and theater critic Ben Brantley, might open up an entire new genre for students and help them see that writing extends far beyond the academic essay. Moreover, by discussing reviews and other popular texts with students, instructors can help students to explore the concept of genre itself and why the essays they are asked to write in school differ as they do from the texts they read outside the classroom. Once they understand these differences, students may begin to write commentaries that move beyond those seemingly simple opinion statements.

Once the commentary is introduced, it is important to keep it going. This doesn't mean that, every time students read a text, they should also submit a commentary—though that's not a bad idea. Rather, it means that the commentary genre must be practiced to improve. Moreover, students should get used to responding to the texts they read, and in order to become comfortable with the form, they must practice it regularly. Therefore, it is best to assign commentaries with most, if not all, of the texts students read at home.

The commentary is not solely an at-home activity. It is meant to be shared, and while it need not necessarily be read verbatim, it should serve as a student's preparation for in-class discussion. By listening to or hearing the commentaries of the seemingly more advanced writers in their class, unsure student writers can themselves grow as writers, eventually developing more interpretive and analytical commentaries. Most importantly, by writing responses at home that will eventually be incorporated into class discussion, students learn what it means to contribute to an academic conversation—and that their voices as readers, interpreters, and writers of texts have value in the classroom.

CONCLUDING THOUGHTS

Thoughtful text selection is an important criterion of a successful racial literacy curriculum, but it is important for instructors to maintain perspective. This curriculum is not about literary study, and texts should be seen as a means rather than an end. The texts that inspire intense reflection and productive conversation one semester may not work during the next, and instructors should do their best to ensure that their text selections fit the needs and interests of the students in their classrooms.

Instructors should also consider which texts have been influential in their own understanding of race and racism and may even want to share with students how those texts shifted their own perspectives (though it is best to do so *after* students have read them to prevent clouding students' impressions). One should never underestimate the role a little instructional vulnerability can play in the classroom, especially one in which emotional, oft-controversial topics are placed front and center.

NOTES

1. Annie Murphy Paul, "Your Brain on Fiction," *New York Times*, March 18, 2012, SR6.

2. Gerald Graff, "Why How We Read Trumps What We Read," *Profession* (2009).

3. See Jack Mezirow, "Learning to Think Like an Adult: Core Concepts of Transformation Theory," in *Learning as Transformation: Critical Perspectives on a Theory in Progress*, eds. Jack Mezirow and associates (San Francisco: Jossey-Bass, 2000).

4. Doug Kellner and Jeff Share, "Toward Critical Media Literacy: Core Concepts, Debates, Organizations, and Policy," *Discourse: Studies in the Cultural Politics of Education* 26, no. 4 (2005).

5. Marion Fay, "Music in the Classroom: An Alternative Approach to Teaching Literature," *Teaching English in the Two-Year College* (2001): 372. See also Mara Lee Grayson, "Race Talk in the College Composition Classroom: Narrative Song Lyrics as Texts for Racial Literacy," *Teaching English in the Two-Year College* 45, no. 2 (2017).

6. Terry Husband, "Using Drama Pedagogy to Develop Critical Racial Literacy in an Early Childhood Classroom," *Perspectives and Provocations* 4, no. 1 (2014).

7. The commercials referenced here are "Tide and Downy: The Princess Dress"; "Campbell's: Made for Real, Real Life"; "Old Navy: Pattern Play"; and "Organic Balance: Real Morning Report."

8. Kathy Nakagawa and Angela E. Arzubiaga, "The Use of Social Media in Teaching Race," *Adult Learning* 25, no. 3 (2014): 107.

9. Sheridan D. Blau, *The Literature Workshop: Teaching Texts and Their Readers* (Portsmouth, NH: Heinemann, 2003), 101.

4

Narrative Song Lyrics

A Text-Based Approach to Racial Literacy

"We learned more from a three-minute record, baby, than we ever learned in school."

—Bruce Springsteen[1]

The previous chapter explores the importance of text selection in the racial literacy classroom; this chapter describes one text-based approach to racial literacy instruction.

MUSIC, LITERACY EDUCATION, AND SOCIAL JUSTICE

Visit a house of worship, a political inauguration, or a national sporting event, and you will see that music and cultural ideology have always been linked. This is in part because music and literacy have always been linked. The oral literate tradition, which employs such techniques as rhythm, rhyme, and meter, not only preserves cultural memory but also models the way memory production works in human behavior. It does this by encouraging individuals not necessarily to memorize verbatim but to abstract from the specifics and remember the structure and framework of narrative. At the same time, the oral literate tradition's use of concrete imagery and rhyme aid in memorization. Because rhythm and rhyme in song can help students both retain information and forge emotional connections to textual material, combining music and literacy instruction contributes to a richer, multilayered learning experience in the classroom.

The classroom has also been a significant venue for the intersection between music appreciation and the development of political awareness and social justice. Social justice educators have suggested that, because "listening to music is an emotional and educational experience that potentially shapes an individual's values, actions, and worldview," songs of all genres can be used in classrooms at all levels of education to expose students to different cultures and encourage cross-cultural communication and understanding.[2] Equally importantly, while students often see literature as purely academic, music is popular and accessible. Because of music's ubiquity in young people's lives, bringing music into the classroom can put students on a level playing field with one another—and with the instructor.

HIP-HOP MUSIC AND CULTURE IN THE ENGLISH CLASSROOM

While music-based instruction is not a new addition to the literature curriculum (scholarship attesting to its efficacy can be traced to the 1960s, if not earlier), a wealth of scholarship in the past two decades has attested to the unique power of hip-hop music and culture to teach composition and literary analysis and to integrate marginalized students into classroom discussion. While originally addressed in secondary classrooms, hip-hop-influenced curricula are gradually making their way into college English courses as well.

Hip-hop-based education (HHBE) is about more than rap music; also acknowledged as significant components of hip-hop culture are breakdance, DJ-ing, and graffiti, as well as, more broadly, the sociopolitical significance of hip-hop music as cultural identity and resistance. Emphasizing hip-hop's roots among urban, African American communities and the political emphasis of much early rap music, many hip-hop scholars contend that HHBE is inherently oriented toward social justice.

Though HHBE educators emphasize the social critiques in hip-hop music and culture, citing artists like Common and Talib Kweli as exemplars of hip-hop's sociocritical positionality, the majority of hip-hop songs—like songs from any genre—to which our students are exposed are not politically but commercially driven. While hip-hop has been said to be culturally relevant for all urban youth, the widespread dissemination of hip-hop culture has led to increased thematic homogenization of hip-hop songs. Although many hip-hop record labels operate under the leadership of Black owners, White-owned corporations still largely oversee the music's distribution. In order to achieve success, many artists have been required to appeal to the stereotypical (and often implicitly racist) expectations of the mainstream (White culturally hegemonic) audience.

Just as a lack of racial diversity in the teaching profession is particularly harmful to students of color who do not see themselves reflected in their instructors, there is danger to a lack of diversity in the texts we bring into the classroom. If students cannot see themselves or their own experiences in the literature they read, then they can become easily alienated from classroom life. For many educators, this is a large part of, if not the primary reasoning for, the inclusion in English language arts (ELA) curricula of noncanonical texts, including hip-hop, that represent the worlds of urban students and students of color. But what, then, happens when the only depictions of Black men and Black women that our students encounter in the classroom are the stereotypes that appear in hip-hop songs, as can occur in the (mis)application of hip-hop-based English education?

Additionally, many Black students may not find their experiences or cultures reflected in these texts at all. For example, while West Indian immigrants may quickly find that they are raced alongside African Americans in the United States, the differences between West Indian and African American behaviors and beliefs make attempts to reach these students through African American culture a prime example of essentialism, regardless of the intentions. Moreover, non-Black students of color may not see themselves represented in the traditional White canon *and* hip-hop texts.

Instructors seeking to employ hip-hop texts ought to thoroughly consider *why* they want to bring hip-hop texts into their classrooms. To rely solely on hip-hop texts would be to assume that students have a vested interest in hip-hop, an assumption that betrays an essentialist perspective on race and culture. On the other hand, if thoughtfully implemented, a hip-hop curriculum can in fact use these texts to encourage students to critique the problems within particular communities, including their own, and to interrogate broader societal ideologies and matters of media representation. A liberatory media pedagogy must look beneath surface representations to analyze the structural and ideological forces with which all media are intrinsically enmeshed. As such, educators seeking to implement music-based curricula (from hip-hop or any other genre) must ensure that their curricula also encourage racial literacy.

To ensure that our media curricula promote multicultural literacy, we must be as critical and discerning in our curriculum development and text selection as we are in our approaches to reading media texts. While the inclusion of hip-hop texts might be very relevant pedagogy for a predominantly African American ELA classroom, it cannot be seen as the go-to curriculum for incorporating media into all literature and composition classrooms, particularly in the diverse community college setting. How, then, can instructors design a relevant media curriculum for the diverse college English classroom that acknowledges students' cultural differences while also creating an inclusive student community?

TEACHER RESOURCE:
THE NARRATIVE SONG LYRICS CURRICULUM

Hip-hop provides one way for teachers to envision a new English education[3]; it is not, however, the only way. Instructors can expand their music-as-text curricula to include songs from other genres of music in addition to, but not in lieu of, hip-hop. This shift calls for a new schema by which to organize these texts to ensure they are not selected haphazardly from instructors' iPods or top-40 radio. To this end, the narrative song lyric curriculum can be seen not as a challenge to hip-hop-based pedagogies but instead an expansion thereof, an attempt to include other genres of music that might more inclusively speak to a diverse student population.

What Are Narrative Song Lyrics?

A narrative can be broadly defined as an account of connected events, organized into some sort of sequence. Narrative can also be understood as a rhetorical approach to arrangement (as opposed to, for example, argumentation). Oral storytelling, fiction, memoir, some journalism, and some poetry, among other genres, employ narrative as a primary mode of discourse. The pedagogical use of narrative literature (traditionally fiction) to engage students both academically and socially is grounded in decades of scholarship. English education pioneer Louise M. Rosenblatt explained that literature enlarges knowledge not because it provides information but because it provides additional experiences for readers: "New understanding is conveyed to them dynamically and personally. Literature provides a *living through*, not simply *knowledge about*."[4]

Though song lyrics are frequently compared to poetry, owing to their use of such poetic devices as meter, rhyme, and repetition, narrative song lyric (NSL) texts resemble short stories and utilize traditional techniques like plot, character, setting, and conflict, just to name a few. Instructors should ensure that the NSL texts they select for inclusion in the curriculum are simultaneously accessible and challenging to the students in the classroom. As such, chosen songs should have literary elements that are clear but not overt or simplistic; there should be some level of ambiguity to encourage students to look closely at the text (see box 4.1).

To ensure texts represent a diverse cross-section of narratives, appeal to students' musical interests, and expose students to songs they might not otherwise have access to, instructors should select songs from a wide variety of musical genres. Of course, some musical genres employ narrative more often than others: folk, country, and rap music, for example, have traditionally employed this discursive approach to tell stories. There are, however, options available from many genres of music (see table 4.1).

Reading NSL Texts in the Racial Literacy Classroom

Students studying the NSL curriculum should read texts through rhetorical and critical lenses. In other words, they should look at the author, implied audience, and contextual factors surrounding the production and reception of the text, as well as who is (or is not) represented in the text—and how those individuals and groups are represented. Lyrics should be read first as written texts, though music may be played following initial textual analysis to invite students to appreciate the overall musical impression and how instrumental elements contribute to the song's meaning. To ensure proper credit is given to writers, instructors should address the difference between the writer of a song text and the performer. Instructors can even use this information to jump-start a conversation about the reasoning behind academic citation.

BOX 4.1. HOW TO DETERMINE
IF A SONG FITS INTO THE NSL CURRICULUM

- **Are there lyrics?** This may seem obvious, but it is worth addressing so as not to diminish the social, cultural, and educational value of instrumental music. While instrumental genres are just as influenced by artistry, culture, and the forces of structural racism, for the purposes of this curriculum, songs must include lyrics.
- **Is there a narrative voice?** This might be a first-person character speaking directly to the audience; a first-person narrator speaking to another person, in which case the "you" addressed may be the audience or an implied other character; a second-person narrator ("you"); or a third-person narrator speaking about other characters and events.
- **Are there characters?** Characters in NSL texts may or may not communicate via dialogue, and they may or not interact directly, but they must all be part of the overarching narrative. Characters may have names; they may not. They may be human beings, but they can also be animals or inanimate objects personified or simply treated as players in the sequence of events the narrative tells. A terrible storm may be the antagonist to the hero's easy journey home. Time or space may be described as the force that prevents two lovers from uniting—or that brings them together.
- **Is there a plot?** An NSL text should have a beginning, middle, and end— sort of. Any of these may be implied or conveyed through flashback or speculation. The story need not be told chronologically, but there should be some sense of movement over time. A narrative tells a series of connected events, however small those individual events may be.
- **Is there specificity or detail of character, setting, or plot?** Specificity and detail turn a plot into a story. Specificity and detail differ: Specifics point to particulars and identify, such as the numerical address of a house; details, like the color of the roof and the condition of the lawn, describe or illuminate. Both of these turn otherwise-bland or mundane sequences of events into fleshed-out narratives we can visualize, feel, and connect with as readers. In an NSL text, a character may have a name or be assigned personality traits; imagery may bring a setting to life; or seeming minutiae of plot can transform the most traditional "boy-meets-girl" tale into a heartbreaking love song.

Table 4.1. A Multigenre Sampling of NSL Texts

Song	Author(s)	Performer(s)*
"Straight Time"	Bruce Springsteen	Bruce Springsteen
"Fast Car"	Tracy Chapman	Tracy Chapman
"The Last Time I Saw Richard"	Joni Mitchell	Joni Mitchell
"Stan"	Marshall Mathers, Dido, Paul Harmon	Eminem (featuring Dido)
"Norwegian Wood"	John Lennon, Paul McCartney	The Beatles
"Hurricane"	Bob Dylan, Jacques Levy	Bob Dylan
"Children's Story"	Slick Rick	Slick Rick
"That Summer"	Pat Alger, Sandy Mahl, Garth Brooks	Garth Brooks
"Brenda's Got a Baby"	Tupac Shakur, Deion "Big D" Evans	2Pac
"Maggie May"	Rod Stewart	Rod Stewart
"Livin' on a Prayer"	Jon Bon Jovi, Richie Sambora, Desmond Child	Bon Jovi
"It Was a Good Day"	Ice Cube	Ice Cube
"Deportee (Plan Wreck at Los Gatos)"	Woody Guthrie, Martin Hoffman	Woody Guthrie (also covered by the Highwaymen, Joan Baez, and others)
"Desperados Waiting for a Train"	Guy Clark	The Highwaymen
"Paradise by the Dashboard Light"	Jim Steinman	Meatloaf (with Ellen Foley and Phil Rizzuto)
"We Are Never Ever Getting Back Together"	Taylor Swift, Max Martin, Shellback	Taylor Swift
"Why Can't You Be"	Stephan Jenkins	Third Eye Blind
"Red Right Hand"	Mick Harvey, Nick Cave, Thomas Wydler	Nick Cave and the Bad Seeds
"A Boy Named Sue"	Shel Silverstein	Johnny Cash
"Dance with the Devil"	Felipe Andres Coronel	Immortal Technique
"Save the Life of My Child"	Paul Simon	Simon and Garfunkel
"Turn the Page"	Bob Seger	Bob Seger (also covered by Metallica)
"It Was a Very Good Year"	Ervin Drake	Frank Sinatra

* There may be numerous performances or recordings of a particular song. In the case that the song was performed by someone other than the songwriter(s), the performer listed denotes the version of the song I selected, unless noted otherwise.

To connect their reading and discussion of NSL texts to the goals of the composition classroom, students should write—a lot. Possible assignments include informal commentaries and responses to NSL texts, character analyses, personal reflections, formal essays, and research-based papers that invite students to consider questions of representation and rhetoric on a broader societal level. More information about these assignments is discussed later in this chapter.

Learning through the NSL Curriculum

When the focus of a curriculum is on text, students—and instructors—may begin to forget that the goals of this curriculum are racial literacy and critical writing, not literary criticism or appreciation. Literacy—not literary—skills and ideas drive this curriculum. As such, instructors must keep in mind the concepts and practices they hope to teach and periodically check in to ensure that discussions and assignments direct students toward that education. The following are some practices encouraged by the NSL curriculum. While some of these practices may occur in the natural course of events, others may need to be introduced and guided by the instructor.

"Real World" Connections and the Limitations of Race Rhetoric

In the racial literacy classroom in which his professor employed the NSL curriculum, James, a Hispanic-identifying community-college student who rushed to class every morning after working the graveyard shift as a hospital orderly, found that he felt a personal connection to one text: "Straight Time" by Bruce Springsteen. The song narrates an ex-convict's struggles to connect with his family and avoid a life of crime. James drew a parallel between the narrator's struggles and those he witnessed in his own New York City neighborhood: "It's the same thing in the 'hood. I see all the time guys try to do good when they get out, but most of the time they wind up going back."[5]

While many of his classmates saw the central conflict of Bruce Springsteen's "Straight Time" as a result of the narrator's poverty, Nicholas, a thirty-year-old returning college student and navy veteran who self-identified as Puerto Rican, saw the problem as more psychological than socioeconomic. He drew on his personal experience as he made sense of the struggles Charlie goes through after his release from prison:

> *I don't think it necessarily has to do with prison at all. I think it's a mind-set thing. I mean, cause—and I'm gonna throw a little personal information out there—but like me, I have PTSD. When I came back from the military, I haven't been the same, and I deal with a lot of personal issues, and I know that the mind-set, it's everything in my mind, but I feel like I'm in this sort of bubble. So I think that with this particular story, it's just a mind-set.*

The openness of the story songs featured in the NSL curriculum encourages students to fill in gaps[6] left unsaid and to challenge one another on their differing interpretations of the characters and events described in the narratives. Students in the racial literacy classroom should be asked to support claims they make with evidence from the texts; knowledge they have gathered elsewhere, such as in other classes they have taken or from stories they have read in the newspaper or seen on television; and situations they have experienced firsthand. They should also then reflect on the ways in which these extratextual connections influence their interpretations of texts.

Nicholas's statement about the central conflict of "Straight Time" demonstrates his recognition that his interpretation of the narrator's struggle is grounded in his own experience with post-traumatic stress disorder. To help Nicholas develop a fuller understanding of positionality and situatedness, his instructor should encourage him to consider how this personal experience both affords him a unique lens on the characterization of Charlie and limits his ability to accept other interpretations of Charlie's struggle.

James shares a different connection to "Straight Time." He claims that he sees a similar dynamic to the one Springsteen describes in the former prisoners he knows from his own neighborhood. By pointing out the difficulty of going "straight" after being released from prison, James demonstrates that he has an understanding of the myriad factors involved in recidivism. More intriguingly, however, by making a connection between the text's narrator, Charlie, who appears to live in a rural area and works in a rendering plant (and whom most students assumed, based in part on these factors, to be White), and the men he sees in his own "'hood" in New York City, James seems to interpret Charlie's struggle as more than a matter of geography or race.

Due to traditional racial discourse, which emphasizes race without acknowledgment of socioeconomic or geographic factors, many students have difficulty imagining that troubles associated with urban life (poverty, recidivism) could also prevail in rural America. The racial literacy framework, however, reminds us that this discourse "masks how much poor whites have in common with poor blacks and other people of color,"[7] a move that is arguably intentional and strategic. James's observation, therefore, is a significant marker of his developing racial literacy. His instructor could then invite him to reflect, in writing or continued class discussion, on the limitations of this racial discourse and the sociopolitical motivations behind such rhetoric. In the racial literacy classroom, students must consider not only how race influences lived experience but also how race *is used* to influence, represent, and interpret lived experience.

Students in the racial literacy classroom can use personal sharing and draw on their lived experiences to make sense of and communicate their ideas about diversity and (in)equity. These impressions, however, must be taken in context. In other words, the specialized knowledge that informs racial literacy must be drawn not only from students' individual experiences but also from immersion in their communities and interaction with those around them.

If students are comfortable enough to share their own experiences openly in the classroom, then they will have more access, through dialogue, to others' experiences and to perspectives that differ from their own. By addressing their own experiences as they relate to the stories they read in the NSL texts—and therefore also their own assumptions and biases—students in the racial literacy classroom are better able to consider ideas and perspectives outside of those boundaries.

Assuming, Confirming, Contradicting, Reflecting

> Having read the lyrics to the song "Straight Time" but not yet having heard the music, many students in the community college classroom studying the NSL curriculum assumed "Straight Time" to be a rap song rather than a piece of folk music, the genre it most closely resembles.
>
> Omar, whose family was from Iran, disagreed: "Bruce Springsteen? I could tell just by the name he's no rapper."
>
> Cora, a young African American woman, nervously explained, "I'm not trying to, like, um, say a statistic or anything, but I mean, guy, prison, you know, how life is—that's kinda what most rappers speak about." A few of her classmates agreed, while others challenged that country music (the genre they many assumed the song to be part of) frequently addressed such topics.
>
> After they heard the song, students began to reflect on their initial assumptions about the story and musical genres. Jim, a White student who grew up in the country, said, "We do tend to associate certain issues with different genres."

Because reflection is such a big part of the racial literacy curriculum, instructors should encourage students to draw on their own experiences as they make sense of NSL texts. However, sometimes students' personal experience with the text or its content can lead them to jump to conclusions based not on full interpretations of the text but instead assumptions and generalizations.

Unlike James, Cora assumes "Straight Time" to be a rap song because of its emphasis on prison and the struggle to build a life after being released. She makes an assumption, seemingly based on other music with which she is familiar, that such a story must belong to the rap genre. In doing so, however, she is also drawing on a racialized assumption about crime: Rap and hip-hop were created largely as a testament to life in poor, urban, Black communities, and by conflating rap and crime, Cora seems to identify crime as a Black problem. However, Cora hedges her statement ("I'm not trying to"), seemingly in an attempt to avoid offending anyone, which demonstrates that she knows she is making a generalization. Rather than allowing conversation to continue unchecked, this would be a good space for the instructor to step in and ask Cora—and her classmates—why she believes this generalization holds true in society.

Having an assumption is not in itself a problem; not being able to identify an assumption as such, however, is. Students must acknowledge the assumptions they hold about society, particularly where race is concerned, and then do the work—through reading, talking, and reflecting—of examining whether that assumption holds true. Other aspects of NSL texts that may provoke students to assume (and therefore invite students to explore their assumptions) are the language the writer uses (including word choice, syntax, and dialect); the writer's name (especially if it seems to point to the author's gender, race, or ethnicity); and, once students hear the song, the performer's voice, including accent and style.

Are all generalizations problematic? To some extent, media must generalize, just as writers must generalize, in order to appeal to an audience. At the same time, however, these generalizations become increasingly problematic when they do not reflect the lived experiences of real people. Conversations that result from the reading of NSL texts not only demand students reflect on their own assumptions about music but also may provoke a more critical discourse about how media reifies, responds to, and perpetuates racial stereotypes.

Critical Media Literacy and Responding to Stereotypes

> Peter, a White physical therapy student who had worked in marketing in the twenty years prior to returning to college, was especially intrigued by the balance of vagueness and specificity with which Springsteen writes in "Straight Time." With regards to the setting, Peter noted, "It seems like it takes place in a rural area, but he never actually says where it is."
>
> "I think the story would have been clearer if he'd said where it takes place," said Anthony, a Black graphic arts student. "I'd be able to picture it better."
>
> Rosie, a Puerto Rican psychology student, suggested Springsteen might have left the place unnamed in order to appeal to a diverse audience and encourage the listener to draw their own connections to the text: "Maybe he left it open-ended for different people to relate to it? If he says the specific place, only specific people can relate, but if it's open-ended we can use our imagination."
>
> Peter, however, saw the matter as more pragmatic than artistically motivated: "It could get more commercial airplay if he doesn't specifically state that state. You don't hear 'New York, New York' in California on commercial radio. From a marketing standpoint, it may make sense to be ambiguous."

In this example, Peter draws on his experience in marketing to point out that all media are driven by financial as well as creative concerns. This is a particularly significant component of the NSL curriculum. All media present messages to their audience, regardless of whether that audience recognizes the messages being transmitted. It is important that teachers who use media in the classroom encourage students to recognize this fact because of the inherent power structures involved in media construction and dissemination.

A particular song may seem to be the work of an artist, but songs make their way to the public through radio and other media outlets in part because of artistry but more because those particular songs were deemed profitable. For example, if a duet is played on the radio and sells very well, it is likely that more duets will soon be played on air. Music follows consumer trends, as well as musical ones. This is troublesome where seemingly countercultural music movements like hip-hop are concerned, given that dominant social and economic groups are largely responsible for their creation and distribution. Artists who buck the mainstream instrumentally or whose lyrics challenge existing hegemonic structures may receive less airplay than those who put forth familiar, marketable, and more sociopolitically innocuous songs. Success, therefore, is at least in part dependent on maintaining the status quo.

By discussing the role of marketing in artistic and media production, students can examine the ways media perpetuate racial, ethnic, and geographic stereotypes to ensure mass appeal and increase sales. Instructors can ask students to consider how their favorite songs or the genres of music they most often listen to represent people. Often, individuals are drawn to music that is familiar and in some way illustrative of their own lives or that showcases something they want but don't have. When students reflect on their favorite NSL texts, they learn more about stories, media, and themselves.

Authorial Choice

In the example in the previous section, Peter wonders if Springsteen's approach to setting is influenced by commercial rather than creative concerns. Rosie, on the other hand, sees the vagueness of setting in "Straight Time" as a rhetorical choice the author has made to engage his audience. While media are driven both by artistic and economic demands, Rosie's interpretation points to the interplay between audience and authorial choice in crafting a text.

It is worth noting that, in situations like this, students in the racial literacy classroom may raise questions to which they never receive complete answers. The actual reason(s) Springsteen left the setting vague is likely unanswerable and beyond the scope of the curriculum. More important is the acknowledgment of the many possible answers, especially as that acknowledgment encourages students to consider the possible paths they can take in their own writing. While Rosie seems to see Springsteen's vagueness as an effective mode of engaging the audience, Anthony finds the lack of specificity off-putting as a reader. It becomes clear for students, then, that certain approaches are better suited to particular audiences.

By postulating reasons an author has made a rhetorical choice, students begin to imagine scenarios in which they might do the same or employ a different approach. It can be very helpful here for instructors to turn the conversation toward students' conceptions of rhetoric and the writing process by asking one deceptively simple question: "What would you have done?" By inviting students to step out of their reader shoes and try on the role of writer, instructors encourage students to develop a rationale behind the choices they might make as writers; in a sense, students can begin to develop their own theories of writing.

INSTRUCTIONAL STRATEGY:
THE "REAL-WORLD" TEXTUAL ANALYSIS

"The more I try to look at it from one lens, the more it seems like it's not just about race. It's about race, but it's also about gender and poverty."

—Amy (White)

At some point in any critical-writing classroom, formal papers must be assigned. Generally, a formal paper in a college writing class incorporates argumentation and research. One assignment that has been found to be successful in the racial literacy classroom draws on English educator Deborah Appleman's work in secondary English language arts. Appleman has argued that, by learning to identify and critique the ideas and underlying ideologies of literary texts, students are better able to apply those techniques to the social, cultural, and political events they encounter outside the classroom.[8]

In the real-world textual analysis paper, students take the critical literacy skills they have learned in the racial literacy classroom and apply them to a situation they have witnessed or experienced in their own lives. Depending on the class, instructors can direct students to analyze that situation using the components of the racial literacy framework, or they can invite students to employ a more traditional critical lens— Marxist theory, feminist theory, or postcolonialism, to name a few—as they analyze the chosen real-world text.

For example, if a man and a woman are seen arguing on a public street, a student viewing the argument through a feminist lens might suggest that the man is resisting the woman's attempts to assert herself. Another student might employ a cultural studies perspective and point out that, while in some communities arguing on the street is seen as an inappropriate airing of private business, in others, people consider community to include more than the nuclear family. The gender scholar or queer theorist might add that there is no guarantee this man and woman are involved in a romantic relationship or might examine how each performs or resists a public role defined by gender.

Racial literacy is not itself a critical lens (though it is influenced by critical race theory, which *is* one such lens), but by using critical lenses to interrogate such individual aspects as class, gender, and geography, students can begin to consider the ways in which race constantly interacts with other individual, social, and demographic variables. Moreover, the assignment calls for students not only to examine the interplay between these variables in one individual situation but also to consider how that situation might be representative of broader structural ideology, hierarchy, inequity, or any combination of the three.

For students who are unsure where to begin analyzing a text, printed or experiential, the assignment can provide a point of entry. For other students, like Amy, who find it difficult to extract one single thread or line of inquiry from the text, this assignment can provide the boundaries needed to focus. For all students, this assignment invites consideration of how a critical lens contributes to the reading of literary work, including its benefits and limitations.

If instructors choose to invite students to consider multiple perspectives rather than limit the assignment to the racial literacy framework, care should be taken to ensure that students understand what is asked of them. Because the racial literacy classroom is not about literary analysis per se, it is unlikely that instructors will have spent a great deal of time on critical lenses, such as Marxist or feminist theory. As such, it is important that instructors provide some information on each of these lenses prior to assigning the formal paper. It might also be useful to provide a "cheat sheet" of sorts listing important elements of selected critical lenses.

CONCLUDING THOUGHTS

Rather than providing information, narratives, whether in literature, on screen, or in song, invite students into the experiences they relate. Because narratives tell stories of real or imaginary people, discussions of race may emerge naturally—or with some careful direction from the instructor—through the analysis of lyrical song texts. By analyzing the ways race plays out in story songs and how it has influenced the crafting, dissemination, and interpretation of those stories, students use these texts as the starting point for the practice of racial literacy. Their identification with characters and events in the story songs, as well as the common ground they may find with one another through extended textual analysis and discussion, can expose societal problems of racism, representation, and inequity, as well as the limitations of sociopolitical racial discourse.

Additionally, because media influences the way students—and educators—make sense of race and racism, critical media literacy is an intrinsic part of racial literacy. The NSL curriculum encourages the development of critical media literacy and rhetorical awareness by asking students to critically analyze the messages within individual songs, consider questions of authorship and audience, and challenge their preexisting impressions of musical genres. By reading in the classroom texts that are often consumed outside of the classroom, students become better equipped to respond to the media messages to which they are exposed in their daily lives, in school and once they walk past classroom doors.

NOTES

1. Bruce Springsteen, "No Surrender," *Born in the U.S.A.*, Columbia Records, 1984.
2. Denise L. Levy and Daniel C. Byrd, "Why Can't We Be Friends? Using Music to Teach Social Justice," *Journal of the Scholarship of Teaching and Learning* 11, no. 2 (April 2011): 64.
3. David E. Kirkland, "'The Rose That Grew from Concrete': Postmodern Blackness and New English Education," *English Journal* 97, no. 5 (2008): 69.

4. Louise M. Rosenblatt, *Literature as Exploration*, 5th ed. (New York: Modern Language Association of America, 1995), 38.

5. All examples in this chapter are real discussions that emerged from the reading of one NSL text, "Straight Time" by Bruce Springsteen, used to illustrate the multitude of learning opportunities that may arise from any given NSL text. For more, see Mara Lee Grayson, "Race Talk in the College Composition Classroom: Narrative Song Lyrics as Texts for Racial Literacy," *Teaching English in the Two-Year College* 45, no. 2 (2017).

6. Wolfgang Iser, *The Act of Reading: A Theory of Aesthetic Response* (Baltimore: Johns Hopkins University Press, 1978).

7. Lani Guinier, "From Racial Liberalism to Racial Literacy: *Brown v. Board of Education* and the Interest-Divergence Dilemma," *Journal of American History* 91, no. 1 (2004): 114.

8. Deborah Appleman, "What We Teach and Why: Contemporary Literary Theory and Adolescents," *Minnesota English Journal* 43 (2007).

5

Emotion Is Everything

Feeling and Experience in the Racial Literacy Classroom

"Not every moment in the classroom will necessarily be one that brings you immediate pleasure, but that doesn't preclude the possibility of joy. Nor does it deny the reality that learning can be painful. And sometimes it's necessary to remind students and colleagues that pain and painful situations don't necessarily translate into harm."

—Ron Scapp[1]

Racial literacy involves more than the provision of information; it is an ongoing practice that, while reflective and analytical, must also be embodied and emotionally driven. Considering emotion, however, may at first seem to composition instructors like messy—or even dangerous—territory. Instructors have departmental mandates to deal with, not to mention limited in-class time, which may take precedent over the emotional lives of the many students in the classroom. For adjunct and nontenured faculty, the pressures may be even greater: Knowing that contractual renewal or promotion depend on the fulfillment of course requirements and positive evaluations from students and other faculty members, instructors may be reluctant to bring sensitive or potentially controversial material into the classroom.

Emotion may initially seem better left to the social worker or the psychologist—but anyone who has spent time in the classroom face to face with twenty or more students from different familial, educational, and cultural backgrounds knows that emotion is *always* a component of classroom dynamics.

For the teacher of adult students, a wide range of emotional concerns may come into play in the classroom. On residential campuses, lowerclassmen and students away from home for the first time may experience homesickness; this can be even more pronounced when classroom material encourages students to reflect on their past experiences. The first-year college experience may also be accompanied by emotional upheaval around matters like friendship, dating, and carving out a new individual identity for oneself, not to mention academic and career concerns. On nonresidential campuses, particularly in two-year and community colleges, students bring additional baggage to the classroom: Older and returning students may have full-time jobs, familial or child-care obligations, or financial concerns that interfere with their studies; international students, recent immigrants, and military veterans also bring complex emotional lives to the classroom.

Regardless of the emphasis in Western education on empiricism over experiential reality,[2] the classroom can never be an emotion-free space. For the composition instructor, especially one interested in the practice of racial literacy, the abundance of opportunities for emotional engagement is best seen as a blessing rather than a burden.

The composition instructor is in a unique position to engage students on an emotional level through the reading of published texts and the craft of original writing. Because literature deals with narrative and human experience, it offers students the potential to grow as individuals and members of a community rather than only as scholars. Academic writing, too, is well suited to emotional engagement in the classroom. While some students may have learned that academic discourse ought to be objective, college composition instructors can encourage students to see that research and academic writing are always filtered through an individual writer's voice.

One's own understanding of the world greatly influences how he or she perceives, interprets, and shares information. By working through problematic situations—real or fictional—and feeling the emotions (negative or positive) that arise therefrom, students are better able to forge connections with curricular materials. This is especially important when we hope to engage students' emotional understandings of race, racialism, and racism.

The role of emotion in racialism and racism is not limited to the negative feelings that arise when one is subjected to overtly racist acts or speech. Because the systemic structures of race are salient in ways apparent and invisible, racialism and racism are intrinsically emotional in ways so deeply entrenched that they are often unrecognized.

In the classroom, the emotional norms and values that undergird curricular and pedagogical decisions determine the nature and structure of race talk. Our classrooms, after all, are subject to the same structural forces and ideologies—racial, racist, and otherwise—that influence all aspects of society. Those values, whether they are indirectly influential or are directly espoused by teachers and administrators, can do more than influence the tone and direction of race talk—they can silence it. In some cases, the emphasis school culture places on positivity and a "good attitude" can inadvertently perpetuate meritocratic ideologies that silence any discussion of racism; in this context, addressing inequity may be seen as "complaining."[3]

In addition to illustrating the significance of considering school culture when designing a racial literacy curriculum (see chapter 2), situations like this demonstrate the need for instructors and students to acknowledge just how much feelings and emotional norms influence language and behavior around race on and off school campuses. As such, composition instructors working within the racial literacy framework ought to encourage students to consider their own emotive contexts and, then, to readdress those contexts with a critical eye. Because structural inequities are enacted in individual contexts, addressing individual emotions helps students to recognize that their feelings and lived experiences do not exist in a vacuum but instead highlight larger societal norms with regards to race and racism.

EMOTIVE CAPACITIES OF RACIAL LITERACY

In order to build racial literacy skills, one must begin to develop a set of key emotive capabilities: broadening one's capacity for compassion and empathy, voicing one's feelings and experiences, attentively listening, and learning to tolerate frustration.

Expanding Compassion and Empathy

"I feel like sometimes, people feel no connections to each other."

—Mimi ("blended")

Just as race is emotionalized, emotion is raced. Individually experienced emotions attain much of their meaning from the sociocultural contexts in which they occur.[4] Emotional contexts are often so deeply ingrained that individuals do not even realize how contextual factors have contributed to their understanding of language, text, and personal identity, let alone to matters of race and racism.

The way a student reacts to a text or a statement made in the classroom is influenced not only by the emotional norms of the classroom but also by that student's cultural influences and past experiences. Even the definition of a piece of emotional terminology may differ between students based on their cultural and language practices, to the point where one student's understanding and experience of anger or fear may differ from another's. More troublingly, individuals' emotions are often raced in essentialist ways: consider, for example, stereotypes of the "angry Black woman" or the "passionate Latin lover." It is imperative that students in the racial literacy classroom are given the space to express emotion without fear of being silenced or stereotyped.

To ensure a respectful environment, teachers should discuss with their students early in the semester a policy or set of guidelines for in-class conversation. Instructors may include this policy in the initial course syllabus or write it with their students as an in-class activity. It is best that students be included in the process either by helping to develop these guidelines or by being invited to voice their concerns about a policy the instructor has introduced.

These guidelines should not be seen as hard and fast rules but as a flexible framework that can be discussed and modified as the semester progresses and students get to know each other better. Guidelines need not adhere to political correctness but should be developed with consideration for the student population, the school culture, current events, and up-to-date scholarship on race and pedagogy. Box 5.1 is an example of a policy statement that can be included on the course syllabus.

BOX 5.1.   SAMPLE RESPECTFUL HONESTY POLICY FOR A SYLLABUS

As many of the topics we will discuss in the classroom may be sensitive and/ or controversial in nature, it is expected that all students will treat one another with the utmost kindness and respect. At the same time, however, I advocate an honesty policy, which means that you are encouraged to share your thoughts and feelings on these topics in the most truthful way with which you feel comfortable. We will explore this policy in greater detail during the first week of class.

Even for individuals raised in racially diverse environments, cross-race impressions are influenced by essentialist representations in popular culture, news media, and politics. However, as students discuss the functions of race with their peers week after week in the classroom, they begin not only to see how racism affects individual people—in both similar and different ways—but also to move past essentialist or stereotypical impressions of people of other races. To this end, one of the most valuable components of the racial literacy curriculum is community. Small work groups and peer-sharing activities help create community in the classroom by inviting students to talk about themselves without the pressure of having to share with the entire class or the instructor. This is a good way for students to get to know people they might not typically befriend outside of the classroom.

One can never truly know what it means to walk in another's shoes—that in itself is a significant point for students to recognize. That said, cross-race dialogues (as well as dialogues across gender, ethnic, and socioeconomic lines) may help students see that individuals are far more complex, emotionally and experientially, than the raced representations generally available through mass media. Through sharing with people of other races, they may even find that, despite distinct cultural contexts, they share similar emotions. Through these small classroom communities, students broaden their capacities for compassion and empathy, emotive capabilities that are integral to the rest of the racial literacy curriculum.

Feeling, Voicing, Counternarrating

During an in-class conversation about recent incidents of police brutality in New York City, the professor asked how many students felt directly affected by these incidents. Most students said they didn't feel a personal connection; a few students shared that they had been stopped on the street by police officers. Cora, a Black-identifying woman from rural Georgia, began to cry. Her professor asked if she would like to share the feelings that had come up. Cora wiped her eyes with a tissue a classmate had offered and shared the following:

> It affects me because I have a son. I don't live in a rich neighborhood. And when somebody looks at my son when I step out of the house—he's Black. So, when I see that cops are killing kids who are unarmed, it's like, what do I do as a mother? How can I prevent that from happening to my son? But there's nothing that I can do. If I teach my son how to fight back, if I teach my son how to have respect for people, it doesn't matter what he do. As soon as he walks out of that door, he's now a responsible—his responsibility is now the streets. The streets now have him, and when he gets older, I'm not gonna be able to be there 24/7 to protect him and that scares me. So it really hits home when I see these kinds of things. It really does. And honestly, it's really scary. I don't want to have to live my life in fear that, if my son gets older, it doesn't matter how he's dressed, it doesn't matter what school he goes to, it doesn't matter how articulate he is, just for the mere fact that he's Black, he could be targeted by police officers.

Through sharing, Black students have the opportunity to command attention and direct the focus of conversation, an opportunity too rarely afforded people of color inside or outside the classroom. Counterstorytelling, a core concept of critical race theory,[5] allows people of color to voice their realities and invites others to glimpse how those realities differ from the stock narratives about race generally forwarded through dominant social discourse. (For more on counterstorytelling, see chapter 6.)

The emotional significance of telling these stories cannot be understated; for people of color who may feel alone in their experiences with racism, voicing these stories may reveal that others have had similar experiences. While this cannot alleviate the pain of racism, it can abate some of the isolation that results from marginalization. Further, by naming the discrimination one has experienced, it is made tangible, and individuals may feel greater hope of eventually combatting it.

While there is a tendency to conceive of racism as functioning solely within a Black/White binary, non-Black groups of color have been racialized and minoritized throughout history. Adding to that complexity is the fact that racism has never been a uniform project; many of those who are racially labeled as White,[6] such as Jewish and Arab people, have been and continue to be victims of racism. Given this Black/White binary, non-Black people of color may feel excluded from many conversations about race and racism.

Moreover, this socially constructed binary conception of race increasingly fails to reflect the population of citizens in the United States of America, particularly in major metropolitan areas. As such, counternarrating is especially significant for students who do not identify as Black or White but have been subjected to marginalization and minoritization as a result of their race, ethnicity, or socioeconomic status.

Sharing emotionally charged experiences with race and racism is not necessarily an easy or painless process. Recalling situations in which one has experienced racism may bring up feelings of pain, anger, and hopelessness. One may feel newly victimized as he or she revisits these memories or disappointed by the reactions of his or her classmates. (Strategies teachers can use to address such negative feelings in the classroom are discussed later in this chapter.) Despite the negative emotions that may arise, experiential knowing and sharing is an integral part of successful race talk. It is important to remember that systemic racism makes itself evident in individual situations; therefore, the individual stories students share serve to illuminate broader societal inequities.

This sharing is even more significant when we consider that personal experience is more often than not discouraged in academic discourse. Given that the United States' educational system and accompanying academic protocol are largely based in the empirical realities of Western science, "experiential reality is not considered as reliable and valid information because it is contaminated by opinions, idiosyncratic experiences, emotions, and personal values."[7] This experiential knowing, however, is an integral part of successful race talk, in part because it makes room in discourse for non-White communication styles. While the racial literacy curriculum alone cannot reconfigure the entire body of Western educational norms, by making the course culturally relevant, both in content and pedagogy, for a diverse population of students, instructors can begin to bridge the gaps that remain between educational institutions and the students they serve.

It is important to note that, while many of these stories may be shared in the racial literacy classroom, some culturally situated communication styles, such as Asian and Asian American discursive norms, which emphasize collectivism and indirectness over confrontation and emotive expression, necessitate that these stories be written rather than spoken. The instructor, therefore, must ensure that students are invited, rather than compelled, to share aloud during in-class conversations and must also provide ample opportunity for written reflection, both inside the classroom and from the privacy of one's own home.

Learning through Listening

A White-identifying community college student named Kevin initially seemed to approach the racial literacy curriculum in his composition class rather skeptically. Tall, older than the average college student, and with a very deep voice, he had a commanding presence in the classroom, and when he spoke, it was usually in short, declarative statements, frequently to point out the complexity of the subject of discussion: "It's hard to say what you would do in the situation."

Often, however, he sat back and observed classroom dynamics rather than actively participating in discussion. As the semester progressed, it became clear that

Kevin's behavior was less aloof than it was attentive. He listened, asked questions to clarify points his classmates made, and verbally acknowledged when he thought one of his classmates had made a good point. However, during a discussion of police brutality, he admitted that, while he believed police violence to be a serious problem, he did not feel personally affected by it.

Just a few moments later, his classmate Cora shared her fears that her Black son would be targeted by police officers. The entire classroom was silent as the students seemed to process the emotional weight of Cora's story. After a few moments, it was Kevin who responded: He softly thanked Cora for sharing, and then he looked down at his desk.

White students in particular may benefit from hearing the emotionalized stories of their classmates of color. Through listening, White students may begin to see that racism is not an abstract social concept but a lived experience that causes real emotional upheaval. Telling White students about race and racism is not enough to begin the process of racial literacy development; instead, the lived realities of race must be emotionally understood.

For students who have not been aware of the effects of systemic racism on their daily lives, one of the first steps of racial literacy involves turning the gaze outside their own perspectives and understanding the lived realities of others. By hearing these stories not as ideas but as first-person narratives told in real time, the influence of racism becomes embodied and tangible rather than intellectual or abstract. They are then more prepared to "move from seeing themselves as innocent and raceless to understanding and experiencing themselves as raced/White."[8]

In the situation described here, Kevin, who has previously approached much of the curriculum with remove, seems to experience a significant shift with regards to his emotional understanding of race and racism. Until this moment, Kevin's awareness of race has been intellectual rather than embodied—in essence, for Kevin, race was something that existed outside of his experience. Upon hearing a classmate describe how police brutality has affected her emotionally, Kevin seems to understand the gravity of these feelings—and the significance of her sharing them with her classmates.

While Kevin's brief expression of appreciation for Cora's sharing may seem small in comparison to the amount of work that needs to be done to improve racial equity, instructors ought to continually remind themselves that racial literacy does not always involve big steps or broad shifts in consciousness. When White students *are* cognizant of race and racism but have yet to understand their own connection to these systemic forces, part of the work of racial literacy is to draw out emotive responses through attentive listening to those who have more directly experienced the effects of race and racism. Broadening the capacity for listening to others' emotional experiences allows students to see the differences and similarities between others' experiences and their own. They are then better prepared to turn that awareness inward to examine the roles race and racism have played in their own lives.

Tolerating Frustration and Ambiguity

> Mira, a public community college student studying a racial literacy curriculum in First-Year Composition, confessed to her professor at the end of the semester that the racial literacy curriculum had made her increasingly cognizant of her own feelings, specifically the discomfort and fear she had always felt around Black men. A light-skinned biracial young woman who identified as "half-Black," Mira grew up primarily with the White side of her family. However, she was keenly aware of the discrimination she had experienced as a non-White woman—in her racial autobiography, she reflected on how hurt she was when her Korean-born boyfriend ended their relationship, citing his parents' objections to what he vaguely referred to as their "cultural differences."
>
> Mira admitted that, while the racial literacy tools she learned allowed her to better understand the ways she had internalized discrimination, they had also led to a fair amount of frustration. "I can't watch the TV," she said, "without seeing how many Black men are portrayed as criminals. And all the Hispanic women are maids."

Frustration is one of the most common emotional responses to the racial literacy curriculum, and it manifests in a number of different forms. However, unlike emotional responses of anger, anxiety, and guilt—which can shut down productive conversation and stall the practice of racial literacy—frustration, and learning to tolerate it, is a necessary part of racial literacy.

Frustration in racial literacy generally arises from the unsettling of existing beliefs and narratives individuals hold about society, many of which have been continually reinforced by dominant cultural ideologies. For example, White students may be discomforted by the knowledge that many of the narratives that prevail in White society—meritocracy, color blindness, and the American dream, for example—shield the racial inequities that are deeply woven into the fabric of American life.

As they reflect on their past experiences, White students may struggle with what has been real: Did they earn their achievements, or has their skin color contributed to their successes? Have their parents knowingly reinforced racist stereotypes? Has everything they have known until now somehow been an illusion? For these students, it is important that they are urged to continue to reflect on the positive aspects of their cultural and familial identities, as well as those that have been determined by race. Inviting students to continually voice these struggles, both in writing and among their peers, helps ensure that they will push through the frustration rather than retreat into the safety of denying White privilege.

For students of color and biracial students like Mira, the racial literacy curriculum may enable them to see how they have internalized essentialist stereotypes; such a perspective may be accompanied by pain and confusion about one's own identity. Psychological models of Black identity development maintain that there is a point in the lives of Black individuals when "it becomes impossible to deny the reality that they cannot become an accepted part of 'the White world.'"[9]

For Black and biracial students, the practice of racial literacy may be foremost an identity-building process through which to develop a positive, antiracist Black identity.[10] Instructors of these students may be able to assist the process by providing students with access to Black-produced media and significant symbols of Black struggles. Becoming familiar with positive representations of people of color may help students like Mira both forge a more positive racial identity and more critically respond to the essentialist representations that dominate mainstream media.

Frustration in the racial literacy classroom is not always directly linked to race; sometimes it is a result of the reading and writing practices that define the composition curriculum. Frustrations may arise as students begin to recognize the complex web that, woven together, factors into any story, be it a printed text, real-world observation, or lived experience. These lived tapestries, if you will, are even more difficult to deconstruct when race, so intrinsic to our social institutions and cultural ideologies, is involved.

Because students in the racial literacy classroom are encouraged to consider elements like socioeconomic class and geography as they interpret these experiences, they are able to interrogate the situational factors that influence the way race functions in society. The interrogation of those factors, however, does not necessarily guarantee that students will come to a single interpretation or solution. The lack of clear answers or truths to questions of race and racism may frustrate students, particularly those for whom these concepts and questions are unfamiliar.

However, the "willingness to suspend closure—to entertain problems rather than avoid them" and the "tolerance for ambiguity, paradox, and uncertainty" are key components of strong reading.[11] These traits—and five others—make up the toolbox Sheridan Blau has called *performative literacy*, or, in other words, the characteristics that lead to behaviors that allow students to become strong readers. Strong readers are comfortable accepting the limitations in their understanding; further, "the most productive readers will even sacrifice whatever comfort they may find in a coherent and apparently complete reading to notice discontinuities or possible contradictions in their understanding of a text."[12]

These traits and behaviors are very similar to those employed by individuals as they begin to practice racial literacy. They tolerate the discomfort that arises as they recognize the paradox between the systemic racism and professed postracialism of American society, they sit with the ambiguity of their role in that society, and they sacrifice their own comfort as they begin to identify as racialized individuals. To ensure that students grapple with this frustration and use it to build their racial literacy toolbox rather than allowing it to derail their progress, instructors teaching the racial literacy curriculum must emphasize the benefits of looking at texts and situations from multiple perspectives, encourage students to sit with the discomfort of unknowing, and help them recognize that learning is a continual process of participating without the potential for perfect mastery.[13]

NEGATIVE EMOTIONAL RESPONSES
IN THE RACIAL LITERACY CLASSROOM

As students explore, through self-reflection and dialogue, the relationship between their individual identities and social constructions of race, negative emotions are likely to arise. These responses are labeled "negative" here, not because they are abnormal or unhelpful, but because they are likely to cause discomfort for the students who experience them and confusion for others in the classroom (students and teachers alike) who may be unsure how to address them.

Hopelessness

> "I feel like the situation is just really bleak. We're having the same problems with civil rights that we were having thirty years ago, forty years ago. There were protests then, there was violence then. It just seems like it's just a cycle of repeating all over again. So it's like, what can you, what can people do?"
>
> —Emma (White)

> "We get so used to hearing about things again and again that it just becomes background noise. And we stop caring for it. We say, oh yeah, we should care but we can't do anything about it so we're just going to pass another day."
>
> —Amina (Arabic)

> "Y'all keep saying this is new. This is not new. It's always been like this for us."
>
> —Tanya (Black)

Ideally, racial literacy will do more than increase students' intellectual and emotional understanding of race and racism; ultimately, it ought to move them toward anti-racist action. This can be exceedingly difficult, however, because, once individuals learn how deeply entrenched racism has been in our society, they are likely to grow disheartened. Having acknowledged the depth of institutional racism, they may fear that inequity is inevitable. For students of color who have been forced to grapple with the lived realities of racism, this can compound the feelings of helplessness and anger they have already experienced. The racial literacy curriculum may feel exhausting for students of color, especially in predominantly White classrooms; they may fear that White students will neither understand nor want to help in the struggle toward racial equity.

White students, too, may feel crippled by their increasing awareness. Once they recognize that they benefit from White privilege, they may think there is nothing they can do to assist their peers of color in the struggle for racial equity. They may see themselves as part of the problem rather than part of the solution. At this point, racial literacy educators should introduce White students to the possibility of becoming White allies in the fight against racism. As allies, White students can use their privileged social positioning to advocate for equity while at the same time acknowledging that they do not own that struggle. The White ally identity offers a "restoration of hope," without which "students, both White and of color, become immobilized by their own despair."[14]

It may also be necessary for instructors and students alike to examine how they define antiracist action both inside and outside the classroom. While the word *activism* may bring to mind images of boycotts, strikes, and protest marches, student activism in the twenty-first century may look quite different. Given its influence and visibility, social media, for example, has become a primary site of activism today.[15]

The truth is that, despite passion and dedication, teachers are limited by time, departmental requirements, and resources. It may not be possible to bring students to a protest rally—nor is it necessarily the teacher's role or right to do so. Antiracist action should not be imposed but instead defined and planned by the students in the classroom. Instructors can invite students, through writing and in conversation, to suggest, explore, and even debate steps that might be taken on both individual and societal scales to combat racism. Moreover, instructors can help their students recognize that discourse itself, particularly the reframing of problematic discourses, can affect change.[16]

Guilt

> Halfway through the semester in which he was enrolled in a racial literacy composition class, Andrew, a White-identifying student with a strong work ethic, visited his professor during office hours. Having sent an e-mail the night before to request a meeting, Andrew now appeared to be uncomfortable, fidgeting in his seat and sheepishly looking down at the floor. After minutes of silence, he confessed, "I'm frustrated."
>
> "OK. Why are you frustrated?" the professor asked.
>
> Andrew took a deep breath and proclaimed, "White people kind of suck!"

Once White students begin to understand the differences between their lived experiences and those of their peers of color, they may be able to develop a more critical perspective of what it means to be White in American society. That critical perspective, however, is often accompanied by disillusionment, frustration, and guilt. (While Andrew labeled his feelings as those of frustration—a significant step in the practice of racial literacy—the sentiment he expresses speaks to feelings of guilt.) This is not unusual among White people as they begin to recognize how deeply situated American racism still is and especially that they have, by virtue of their skin color, indirectly been complicit in the maintenance of White privilege. Admitting this "makes one newly accountable."[17]

Too often, rather than inspiring one to take action, guilt can be paralyzing. Guilt may lead to feelings of hopelessness and a resigned belief in the inevitability of the racist system. Even more problematic, White guilt can function as a way for those who benefit from society's inequities to continue to enact their power inside that system. When a member of the dominant group claims responsibility for the systemic injustices done to members of the nondominant group, that person is empowered by his or her agency in the oppression. In this case, the White individual sees himself as someone who has *done* something; by naming himself an agent of the system that oppresses people of color, he automatically relegates people of color to a passive role, thereby reifying the existing racial hierarchy. While a person cannot control the pangs of guilt that gnaw at his stomach, the choice to dwell in that emotion is an attempt to regain agency in a situation that may be beyond his individual reach.

If the White student expressing guilt has individually discriminated against peers of color, he or she must be encouraged to take steps to act differently in the future. This encouragement alone may help to alleviate the feelings of guilt by turning them into antiracist action. The greatest challenge may be for those White students, like Andrew, who are socially conscious but are borne of a corrupt system that has given them, unrequested, an advantage over Black people and other people of color.

Teachers must help these students recognize that there is a system of inequity larger than they are, so large in fact that one often cannot even visualize its maneuverings. The White individual must learn that he is not personally responsible for these systemic imbalances, even while he benefits from them. He must come to see himself as powerless, a passive heir to an unjust system that has been in existence much longer than he has. Only when the White individual admits to this inheritance will he be able to forge a new identity as a White ally in the struggle for racial justice. Because Andrew voiced his guilt over his own White privilege halfway through the semester, he was able to push through this feeling and begin to discover how he, as a White individual, might push back against racism and White privilege.

Anger

It is likely that students in the racial literacy classroom will get angry. They may be angry at society for being inequitable. They may be angry at their families for having shielded them from the harsh realities of the world. They may be angry at their classmates for having made offensive—or seemingly innocuous—comments in the classroom. They may be angry at themselves for being part of a racist system or for having discriminated against others in the past.

Students will get angry. Some might even say they *should* get angry. Anger can be motivating, if it inspires one to antiracist action, or soothing, if bottled-up emotions are finally released. Anger, however, often masks other feelings, like hopelessness and guilt. If a student expresses anger in the classroom, it is important that the emotion be acknowledged and that subsequent instruction examine its root causes. (The writing exercises provided later in this chapter may be especially useful to both quell feelings of anger and explore underlying emotions.) In situations in which a student is angry at another student, it is important that all in the classroom address the cause in order to reassure students that the classroom is a safe and supportive environment.

Denial, Defensiveness, and Boredom

At a certain point, students may feel overwhelmed and attempt to withdraw from the racial literacy curriculum. They may be quieter in class or avoid turning in assignments. While no one should be forced to speak in class, teachers should take note of student disengagement and consider the emotions that withdrawal may be hiding. Like expressions of anger, these attempts to withdrawal often disguise students' deeper emotional and ideological struggles.

Many individuals retain their long-standing faith in cultural ideologies like the American dream and American meritocracy, even when their experiences and observations speak to the inaccuracy of those beliefs. Denial of inequity is in part a coping mechanism—it is, after all, more pleasant and self-gratifying to believe that one will benefit from the labors of his or her hard work rather than by virtue of skin color. For White students, these familiar beliefs are grounding. For students of color, these beliefs provide a sense of hope that might sustain them through the lived realities of racialism and racism.

White students may experience *disintegration*, the conscious yet conflicted acknowledgment of their own Whiteness.[18] The danger at this point is that the uncomfortable individual might attempt to palliate that discomfort by seeking out information that he or she is not complicit in racism or even that racism no longer exists. It is imperative that the White individual continue to receive information that refutes essentialist stereotypes and explores what it means to be White in a society that oppresses people of color.

Black students may begin to blame other Black people for their oppression or attempt to distance themselves from Black culture for fear that their racial identification will hold them back from social and economic success. Asian-identifying students may deny that this curriculum applies to them and avoid identifying as persons of color. Few people, after all, want to be seen as victims. Therefore, the focus of the curriculum at this point must be on helping students recognize the agency and activism of people of color. Instructors should expose all students—not just students of color—to the life stories and experiences of individuals of color who have acknowledged and talked back to racism.

At some point in the semester, there is a strong likelihood that negative emotions unacknowledged or suppressed by students will manifest as boredom. Students may become "sick of talking about race" or attempt to redirect conversation to other topics, such as socioeconomic class or ethnic identity. It is imperative that these shifts be noted, acknowledged, and incorporated into the curriculum. For example, students may argue that socioeconomic stratification is one of the root causes of American inequity. It is true that "all forms of oppression are about the distribution of resources . . . but that does not negate the reality and salience of racism and how it deepens and intensifies the inequitable distribution of resources."[19] As such, teachers and students must consider these forces as they work together to maintain White hegemony in American life.

BOX 5.2.   STRATEGIES TO HELP STUDENTS THROUGH RACIAL LITERACY'S EMOTIONAL STRUGGLES

Acknowledge

There's no way to get around it: Intense emotional experiences can be difficult. It's even harder to share emotions, especially negative ones. The first thing you must do when a student is struggling emotionally is acknowledge that difficulty. If your student has expressed that struggle, thank him or her for sharing. Say that you understand he or she is feeling overwhelmed (or angry or sad). A simple acknowledgment can help your student feel heard and respected in the classroom.

Tip: Keep in mind that acknowledgment in emotional learning does not necessarily mean agreement. In fact, there will be times when you will want to do anything but validate a perspective that you find repugnant. Still, it is important to acknowledge a student's anger, for example, even if you don't understand it or find it misdirected. All acknowledgment necessitates is the recognition that the feeling is real for the student who is feeling it, regardless of logic or fairness. Let feelings be feelings. Then, through inquiry and support, you—and your students—can dig beneath those feelings to uncover the social and ideological impressions that lie beneath.

Inquire

Inquiry is one of the most important tools in the racial literacy educator's toolbox. Asking questions encourages your students to think more deeply about the ideas or feelings they have expressed. Inquiry also helps you to learn more about the struggle a student is going through and, just as importantly, takes the pressure off you to provide the "right" response.

Tip: Question the content, not the expression. If a student expresses that he or she "hates" something, then focus your inquiry on the object of that hatred rather than pointing out that *hate* is a strong word. (Discussion of language itself *must* happen in the racial literacy classroom, but in an emotional moment, pointing out these particulars can be silencing.) And be concrete: An open-ended question like "Why do you hate it?" may lead to shrugs and murmurs of "I don't know." Instead, ask "What do you hate about it?" to invite a more tangible response.

Support

Be available. If a student is struggling in a class session, then he or she may feel overwhelmed or, worse, abandoned when the meeting is over. Offer to stay behind a few minutes or, if you have some place to be, offer to chat later. Additionally, consider providing students with supplemental materials, such as nonmandatory reading, or referring them to relevant pop culture texts, like songs and movies.

Tip: When you offer support or services, be specific. "Feel free to come and talk to me" sounds helpful, but it places the onus on the student to initiate the encounter. This can be hard for a student who is already struggling. Instead, try something like "I'll be in my office this afternoon after one o'clock. Would you like to talk more then?" Setting a specific time but leaving it open for the student to say no may make you seem more accessible.

Refer

You cannot do everything. Be prepared to refer struggling students to campus counseling and wellness centers if the need arises. Ask for help when you need it.

Tip: Some schools have specific guidelines for referring students for counseling or outside services. Familiarize yourself with these resources prior to the start of the semester. It may be a good idea to provide students with this information early in the semester; consider including contact information for resource centers on the course syllabus.

TEACHER RESOURCE: USING WRITING TO EVOKE EMOTION

Given the unpredictability and intensity of emotional responses to race and racism, how can teachers safely and fairly bring emotion into the racial literacy classroom? For the composition instructor, the answer is deceptively simple: through writing. In-class exercises teachers can use to encourage students to think and feel on the page are guided freewriting, "Writing for Full Presence," and "Breathing to Write."

Guided Freewriting

Guided freewriting encourages students to get their initial reactions and ideas onto the page without having to worry about grammar, spelling, or appropriate diction. In freewriting, students write continuously (without picking up their pens or lifting their fingers from the keyboard) and do not pause to edit or revise their work. Guided freewriting begins with a prompt of some sort, such as a text, question, or quote. The following are some brief guidelines for instructors who wish to use freewriting:

1. Explain the procedures for freewriting, and allow students to ask questions or voice concerns. One common question is *What do I do if I don't know have anything to say?* Tell students that, if they have nothing to say, they can write "I have nothing to say" until something else comes up. Alternatively, they can decide on a "filler word" they can write when they feel stuck. It might even be fun to work together as a class to come up with some amusing filler words.
2. Share a film clip, read an excerpt from a written text, ask a question, or write a quote on the board to serve as an initial prompt.
3. Tell students to pick up their pens (or hover their fingers over the keyboard).
4. Set a timer for a designated amount of time. Start small: two or three minutes at most. Later in the semester, when students are more familiar with the activity, you can work up to five or even ten minutes.
5. When the timer goes off, tell students to put down their pens or stop typing.
6. After freewriting, take a few moments to ask students to reflect on their experiences with the activity and then on the writing they completed.

The texts produced during guided freewriting can be used to brainstorm ideas for a reading reflection or a formal essay assignment. Because some students are hesitant to speak in class for fear of having nothing to contribute or even saying the "wrong" thing, freewriting can also serve as a starting point for in-class discussion around emotionally fraught topics.

"Writing for Full Presence"

Designed by racial literacy educator Yolanda Sealey-Ruiz, "Writing for Full Presence" is another in-class exercise that may help students address their feelings around race and racism.[20] As the name suggests, this writing exercise aims to ensure that students are fully present, cognitively and emotionally, in the classroom. Like freewriting, "Writing for Full Presence" (WFFP) emphasizes content and process as opposed to mechanics. Unlike freewriting, WFFP does not require the constant motion of the pen for a predetermined allotment of time. Instead of assigning a prompt, teachers should invite students to write about anything that is weighing on them emotionally or occupying their minds.

One student may use this time to vent on the page about a frustrating commute or an argument with a friend; another may take this an opportunity to reflect on the day or plan for the week ahead. By putting them on paper, students can purge some of the negative emotions or distracting thoughts that prevent them from fully engaging with course material. While it is a good idea to invite students to share the writing they do, such sharing should never be mandatory.

"Writing for Full Presence" is best assigned to students early in the semester at the very beginning of a class session. This timing allows students to write out whatever is distracting them before encountering class material and also acquaint themselves with the frequent written reflection they will do in the racial literacy composition classroom. Over the course of the semester, teachers can—and should—modify the practice to best suit the students in the classroom and that particular day's activities. On occasion, instructors might play music during WFFP or invite students to illustrate their written jottings.

Ideally, WFFP will become a regular practice in the classroom. Not only does it help students to focus, writing for a few minutes at the beginning of every class session gets students into seeing writing as a regular practice writers do to express their own ideas rather than an academic chore only done when assigned. This insight can be invaluable for even the most reluctant of composition students.

"Breathing to Write"

> "Close your eyes. If you're not comfortable closing your eyes, soften your gaze, and look down past your nose. Place one hand on your heart and one on your belly. Notice where in your body you feel your breath. Is the breath in the upper chest? Around the ribcage? In the belly? Notice the quality of the breath—is it shallow or deep? Without changing anything, without judging, just notice. Keep your awareness on the sensation of the breath in your body; with your mind, follow your inhale, and follow your exhale."[21]

This is a variation of a teaching script for a yogic practice called Apa Japa Pranayama, which loosely translates to "repetition with awareness breath." It is intended to draw a practitioner's focus inward toward the self and, through a string of biological processes, engage the parasympathetic nervous system to slow the heart rate and lower blood pressure, two common physiologic effects of anxiety.

After practicing this breath for a minute—longer may cause students new to the practice to lose focus—students are directed to release their palms, gently blink open their eyes, and open their notebooks. The writing need not be about anything in particular—though, of course, a prompt can be provided in accordance with that day's course material. Instructors may even want to use this breath practice before guided freewriting or "Writing for Full Presence." Because of its physiological effects, this practice is especially helpful when emotions like anxiety and anger are high; it can, however, be used whenever instructors feel students need a moment to regroup or reflect.

English education scholar James Moffett, who was a practicing yogi interested in "silencing the mind as a way to enrich what one knows,"[22] suggested that writing is a way of "modifying inner speech"[23] but noted that "in transcribing inner speech we surprise ourselves and think thoughts we have not thought before."[24] By quieting the mind and stilling the body through focused awareness of the breath, student writers momentarily pause in their search for ideas and appropriate language and instead learn to, as poet Robert Frost suggested, "let what will stick to them like burrs where they walk in the fields."[25]

CONCLUDING THOUGHTS

If writing appears an obvious approach to engaging student emotion in the racial literacy classroom, the more complex questions are *how* and *why* personal writing around race works to elicit both emotional and intellectual understanding. By writing their stories, students begin to look inward to examine how their own experiences, ideas, and feelings are situated in societal structures and cultural ideologies. By sharing their stories, students begin to identify the universal emotions that underlie even the most culturally situated stories, which may in turn improve students' ability to empathize with peers of other racial, ethnic, geographic, and socioeconomic backgrounds.

At the same time, they may begin to recognize that different conditions lead to different lived experiences, thereby developing a sense of how beliefs and ideas unlike their own are formed and moving outside the bounds of their own perspectives. The next chapter explores two activities that enable students to begin to identify their own positionality around race and build skills integral both to racial literacy and effective academic composition.

It is important to acknowledge that engaging emotion in the classroom may not always run smoothly or be successful. Students will be uncomfortable; they may call out their peers or challenge their instructor on the logic or legitimacy of the racial literacy curriculum. The most dedicated teachers will question at times if they are doing more harm than good and if their students'—and their own— discomfort is worth it. For this reason in particular, emotive learning is just as significant for instructors as it is for students. (For more on instructor preparation, see chapter 2.)

That said, if the activities in the racial literacy classroom do inadvertently replicate or create an experience in which students are uncomfortable, after which they seek to challenge, through dialogue, racist or essentialist modes of thinking, this should not be seen as a deficit of the racial literacy curriculum. Characteristics of racial literacy include the ability to "challenge undemocratic practices" and "engage in talk even when difficult or awkward."[26] By resisting stereotypes not only hypothetically but also as they play out inside the racial literacy classroom, students are better able to develop their racial literacy skills.

Remember this: Emotions *will* run high. This does not mean something is going wrong in the racial literacy classroom. Instructors can help students learn to harness those emotions and work with them instead of running from them. Emotion is everything in racial literacy because, without developing certain emotive capacities, the rest of racial literacy becomes impossible.

NOTES

1. Ron Scapp, quoted in bell hooks, *Teaching to Transgress: Education as the Practice of Freedom* (New York: Routledge, 1994), 154.

2. Derald Wing Sue, *Race Talk and the Conspiracy of Silence: Understanding and Facilitating Difficult Dialogues on Race* (Hoboken, NJ: Wiley, 2015), 66–67.

3. Jennifer Siebel Trainor, "The Emotioned Power of Racism: An Ethnographic Portrait of an All-White High School," *College Composition and Communication* 60, no. 1 (2008): 97.

4. Batja Mesquita, "Emotions Are Culturally Situated," *Social Science Information* 46 (2007): 411, 413.

5. Richard Delgado and Jean Stefancic, *Critical Race Theory: An Introduction* (New York: New York University Press, 2012), 48–49.

6. While definitions of race are interrogated throughout this book, according to the U.S. Census Bureau, only the following are classified as races: White; Black or African American; Asian; American Indian or Alaska Native; and Hawaiian Native or Other Pacific Islander. For more, see United States Census Bureau, "Race—About," *Census.gov*, last modified July 8, 2013, http://www.census.gov/topics/population/race/about.html.

7. Sue, *Race Talk*, 67.

8. Amy E. Winans, "Cultivating Racial Literacy in White, Segregated Settings: Emotions as Site of Ethical Engagement and Inquiry," *Curriculum Inquiry* 40, no. 3 (2010): 476.

9. Janet E. Helms, "Toward a Model of White Racial Identity Development," in *Black and White Racial Identity: Theory, Research, and Practice*, ed. Janet E. Helms (Westport, CT: Praeger, 1990), 25.

10. France Winddance Twine, "A White Side of Black Britain: The Concept of Racial Literacy," *Ethnic and Racial Studies* 27, no. 6 (2004): 892–93.

11. Sheridan Blau, "Performative Literacy: The Habits of Mind of Highly Literate Readers," *Voices from the Middle* 10 (2003): 20.

12. Ibid., 19.

13. Jean Lave and Etienne Wenger, *Situated Learning: Legitimate Peripheral Participation* (Cambridge: Cambridge University Press, 1991), 35.

14. For more on contemporary student activism, see Cassie L. Barnhardt, "Campus-Based Organizing: Tactical Repertoires of Contemporary Student Movements," *New Directions for Higher Education* 2014, no. 167 (Fall 2014): 43–58; Paolo Gerbaudo, *Tweets and the Streets: Social Media and Contemporary Activism* (London: Pluto Press, 2012); and Tatiana Tatarchevskiy, "The 'Popular' Culture of Internet Activism," *New Media and Society* 13, no. 2 (2011): 297–313.

15. Beverly Daniel Tatum, "Teaching White Students about Racism: The Search for White Allies and the Restoration of Hope," *Teachers College Record* 95, no. 4 (1994): 473.

16. See Norman Fairclough, *Discourse and Social Change* (Cambridge, UK: Polity, 1992); and Rebecca Rogers and Melissa Mosley, "A Critical Discourse Analysis of Racial Literacy in Teacher Education," *Linguistics and Education: An International Research Journal* 19, no. 2 (2008): 107–31.

17. Peggy McIntosh, "White Privilege: Unpacking the Invisible Knapsack," *Peace and Freedom Magazine* (1989).

18. Helms, "Toward a Model," 58.

19. Robin DiAngelo, *What Does It Mean to Be White? Developing White Racial Literacy* (New York: Peter Lang, 2016), 270.

20. Yolanda Sealey-Ruiz, "From Writing for Full Presence to 'Where I'm From': Writing That Builds Community in the Classroom," in *Hip-Hop in the Heartland Annual Teacher Summer Institute* (Madison, WI, 2015).

21. Mara Lee Grayson, "Breathing to Write: Moments of Yoga in First-Year Composition," *Teaching English in the Two-Year College* 44, no. 4 (2017): 450.

22. Regina Foehr, Miles Myers, Donald R. Gallehr, Richard L. Graves, Sheridan Blau, and Betty Jane Wagner, "A Tribute to James Moffett," *Journal of the Assembly for Expanded Perspectives on Literacy* 3 (1997): 2.

23. James Moffett, "Reading and Writing as Meditation," *Language Arts* 60, no. 3 (1983): 315.

24. Ibid., 320.

25. Robert Frost, "The Figure a Poem Makes," in *The Best American Essays of the Century*, eds. Joyce Carol Oates and Robert Atwan (Boston: Houghton Mifflin, 2000), 178.

26. Amy Vetter and Hannah Hungerford-Kressor, "'We Gotta Change First': Racial Literacy in a High School English Classroom," *Journal of Language and Literacy Education* 10, no. 1 (2014): 87.

6

Personal Writing and Positionality

How We Know What We Know

"As I narrate these experiences, I begin to understand that I, along with my family, am a participant in this discourse. I am a player in a larger drama, performing the parts culture gives to young White males."

—Norman K. Denzin[1]

"Many critics still don't understand that when we 'confess' we seek the commonality of our experiences, thus adding to the full range of what it means to be intensely human. Fearlessly writing memoir allows us to understand our own life narratives, as well as to learn from those 'others.' The more artfully we write, the more difficult it is to ignore or dismiss our stories."

—Sue William Silverman[2]

While people tend to think of themselves as unique—which, to some extent, they are—everyone is influenced by the cultural contexts of both the larger society and the smaller families and communities of which they are a part. Identifying and unpacking these influences is an integral part of the racial literacy curriculum. For example, while an individual student may not think of herself as racist, she must acknowledge that her beliefs about race are influenced by her social positioning in a society in which race plays a major role in determining one's opportunities. For students to address systemic racialization and racism, they must accept their own participation in these systems.

Moreover, examining the relationship between their individual experiences and beliefs and the broader ideologies by which those ideas and experiences are influenced can help students explore the role of narrative as well as rhetorical concepts of author, audience, and context in both storytelling and academic writing. The most important step in this component of the racial literacy curriculum is the exploration of one's own positionality with regards to race, racism, and racialism.

WHAT IS POSITIONALITY?

Positionality, a term traditionally associated with social science research and ethics, broadly means the way an individual is situated in society with regards to social identifiers like race, gender, socioeconomic class, and other cultural categories. It may at first seem obvious that an Asian American, middle-class woman with a graduate degree occupies a different social space than does a wealthy White man who inherited his family business or a working-class Latino laborer. However, an in-depth consideration of individual positionality goes beyond locating oneself in society to also exploring how one has come to occupy that space and how that space influences one's perspective on text, social interaction, and society.

Positionality is a helpful reminder that what is *normative* in society may not feel normal or typical for everyone. One's ideas, beliefs, and interpretations of texts or situations are directly or indirectly influenced by one's own past experiences in the world. Positionality's influence on interpretation is most easily seen where intensely emotional situations are involved.

For example, students reading a short story in which the main character commits suicide might emerge with not only different interpretations of the story but also different feelings about the protagonist. A student who was raised Catholic and believes suicide to be a sin might be disappointed with the character and frustrated by the turn of events; a student majoring in psychology might reread the story for signs of emotional turmoil earlier in the text; and a student who has lost a friend or family member to suicide might feel little sympathy for the protagonist and emphasize in interpretation how the character's decision influences his loved ones.

In classroom interaction, the recognition that all knowledge is situated both "empowers and disempowers individual expertise" and may help students become more open to listening to their peers' perspectives.[3] These practices are especially important where potentially sensitive and controversial matters of social (in)justice are concerned. Students must understand their racialized selves rather than assume an identity that exists outside of the process of racialization. This is especially important for White students, who may initially feel little connection to matters of race. For these students, racial literacy will only develop as they emotionally progress to understand their own racialized identities.

AVOIDING ESSENTIALISM

Early in the semester, Dakota, a dark-skinned student in a First-Year Composition class employing the racial literacy curriculum, wrote that, even though people have always seen him as Black, he prefers to identify as Jamaican and Puerto Rican.

Halfway through the semester, during an in-class activity, Dakota and his classmates were broken into small groups to identify and explore the nature of stereotypes. After Cesar, another student in the class, used his own experience and identity as a Mexican man to critique stereotypes of Latino and Latin American men, Dakota said, laughing, "I guess I'll speak as a Black person then." He followed this interjection with a recollection of the anxiety he felt as an adolescent when teams were picked during gym class; he feared that his classmates might assume that, because he was Black, he was also athletic, which he was not.

Like critical race theory, which holds that people of color already possess knowledge of race and racism unavailable to their White peers, racial literacy has been identified as a type of specialized knowledge informed by lived experience. In fact, racial literacy acknowledges that race is often the "prevailing narrative in the lives of racially minoritized individuals and groups."[4] In this understanding, racial literacy is simultaneously developed through experience and intuitively held by those who are racially minoritized.

There is, however, a difference between that experiential knowledge and the critical consciousness that individuals may develop to interpret and challenge racist acts and structures. In other words, by presuming that all students of color possess innate expertise on systemic racism, one risks the conflation of individual experiential awareness and critical awareness. This conflation fails to acknowledge the myriad ways in which systemic racism works on individual people, including and especially people of color.

Essentialism is the denial or flattening of distinctions between subgroups or individual members of racially defined groups in order to create or maintain racial hierarchies.[5] Individuals who experience racism in their daily lives do not necessarily experience or interpret racism in the same ways, regardless of their shared racial identification. Race, racialization, and racism depend on and interact with other demographic factors, such as socioeconomic class, gender, geography, and sexuality. Racial identities, too, are not innate but rather developed through experience and socialization.

In the situation described here, Dakota explains that, when he was younger, he had been concerned about others' perspectives of him based on stereotypes associated with the color of his skin. Is he now, again, concerned that others expect him to speak as a Black person and does he therefore feel pressured to do so? Is he celebrating or critiquing Cesar's use of personal experience to challenge stereotypes? Is it possible that the racial literacy classroom replicated that essentialist thinking even as the students actively spoke against essentialism?

Dakota simultaneously takes on and resists the Black identity. Having long recognized through lived experience that he was seen as Black despite his multiethnic self-identification, he claims that identity in order to critique the racist, essentialist stereotypes that so often accompany it. At the same time, however, his increasingly critical academic awareness of the function of race and racism in American society allow him to perform that identity, even if he does not identify solely as Black. In other words, he takes on this Black identity not only because he knows that others have assigned it to him but also because he wants to offer a counternarrative to a stereotypical rhetoric of Blackness.

Because it encourages individuals to identify the unique confluences of their experiences and identities, positionality is an important tool to help students see that identity is intersectional and that experience and expertise are not synonymous. In short, one Black man should not be expected to speak for all Black men, but he can use his experiences as a socially identified Black man to respond to existing narratives about Black men.

The genre of memoir has always been associated with a "reform impulse, a railing against the political by trotting forth the personal."[6] When an individual senses that sociopolitical discourse around a particular subject has not addressed her own experiences, through telling her own story, that individual can talk back to correct or expand on that discourse. In this view, stories themselves have the power to transform existing ideologies and discourses around race and identity. In the racial literacy classroom, by encouraging students to talk back to essentialist stereotypes, instructors not only make room for self-expression but also position the personal narrative as a genre of writing that can make a valuable contribution to our academic understandings of race and identity.

TEACHER RESOURCE: THE RACIAL AUTOBIOGRAPHY

In research, positionality is often connected to *reflexivity*, the practice of examining one's own conceptual biases and assumptions about the research and how those biases influence interpretation. As such, exploring positionality requires students to adopt a layered, metacognitive approach to self-reflection: Students must both ask *What do I think about this?* and *What might influence that perspective?* They must ask *How do I feel about this?* and *Why do I feel this way?*

This might all seem very abstract and heady for students (and teachers), and there is nothing in the racial literacy curriculum that demands teachers inundate their students with terms like *reflexivity*, especially early in the semester. In fact, instructors will likely have more success with implementing activities and assignments that encourage students to more organically begin to practice reflexivity. Students who have not thought at length about race and racism may struggle with identifying and articulating their thoughts and feelings. While the give and take of in-class discussion can be helpful in challenging students' assumptions about themselves and the world, it is not enough for students to engage in conversation.

Students who tend to be vocal in the classroom may dominate discussion and direct the flow of conversation—intentionally or incidentally—while those who tend to be quieter learners may miss out on opportunities for substantive dialogue with their peers. As such, it is imperative that students also put in the work when they are alone, through such activities as freewriting, "Writing for Full Presence,"[7] "Breathing to Write,"[8] and informal reading responses.

Through reflective writing, they can begin to talk through their ideas as they write. Not only does this help students begin the self-reflection required in the racial literacy classroom, but it also helps them begin to see that writing itself can be a process of learning.[9] These writing activities also begin to bridge the skills of racial literacy with the foundational concepts of academic composition.

The most significant tool for exploring positionality through writing is one that directly calls on students to address their own identities and beliefs through personal narrative: the racial autobiography. The literacy narrative has long been a mainstay of student-centered composition instruction.[10] For those familiar with literacy autobiographies, it might be helpful to think of the racial autobiography as an expansion or subset of the broader literacy narrative. Rather than recalling their earliest reading and writing experiences, the racial autobiography asks students to begin to reflect on their early experiences reading race and learning about race and racism and to consider how those experiences may have shaped their understanding of themselves, their cultures, and their communities. The structure for the racial autobiography is flexible, and instructors may consider framing the assignment more as a memoir than an autobiography. Consider the distinctions in table 6.1.

Framing the assignment as a memoir may be especially useful for creative writing classes, in which the assignment can function as a first foray into creative nonfiction, or upper-level courses, in which students might already have a deeper understanding of some of the social, cultural, or political ideologies that give meaning to terms

Table 6.1. Autobiography vs. Memoir

	Autobiography	*Memoir*
Subject	An individual of notoriety (e.g., a celebrity or political figure)	Sometimes a writer or celebrity but can be anyone who has experienced something significant
Audience interest in subject	Intrinsic—the audience is interested in the person because of who he or she is	Representative—the subject is of interest because of his or her experience rather than identity
Purpose	A record of a life	A recreation of lived experience
Structure	Generally chronological	Thematic (e.g., organized around a particular event, experience, or idea)

like *race* in our society. For students who are only beginning to interrogate these influences, the assignment may be less thematic than chronological in form, asking students to reflect on a prompt or series of questions. Useful questions include but are not limited to the following:

- How would you respond if someone asked you "What are you?" How do you feel about that question?
- Have you ever been discriminated against? How so?
- Have you ever discriminated against someone else? How so? Why?
- When did you first come to learn about race?
- Was race talked about in your home?
- What does the word *culture* mean to you?
- Did you grow up near people who looked like you, spoke your language, or shared similar customs?
- Have you ever felt out of place because of your race, ethnicity, religion, or socioeconomic class (or some part of your culture, however you define that term)?

Like most components of the racial literacy curriculum, the racial autobiography is highly customizable to best suit the student population and particular course requirements. Box 6.1 presents some important questions to consider when designing the assignment for the racial autobiography.

BOX 6.1. QUESTIONS TO CONSIDER WHEN DESIGNING THE RACIAL AUTOBIOGRAPHY

- **How much do the students already know about race and racial literacy?** Early in the semester, students may feel overwhelmed by an assignment that is too broad or theoretical in nature. They may wonder what you are looking for. As such, it may be a good idea to choose clear, direct personal questions as prompts for students to think about as they write their autobiographies. For example, "Did you or do you now talk about race and racism in your home?" is a more accessible starting point for the new racial literacy student than a question like "How do you feel about the Black/White binary of American racial discourse?"

  If, on the other hand, you are teaching a course for which students are expected to have more background in race studies (e.g., an interdisciplinary or upper-level seminar rather than First-Year Composition), you may want to encourage students to incorporate broader theoretical concepts about race and identity into their personal writing.
- **How rigorous should the guidelines for the assignment be?** Decide in advance how broad or narrow you want the assignment guidelines to

be. Will all questions address race directly, or will you more broadly ask students to consider additional aspects of individual and social identity (regardless of how those factors intersect with race)? If you are working with predominantly White students or students who appear reluctant to address race directly, it might be beneficial to invite students to consider other aspects of identity (such as ethnicity, nationality, socioeconomic class, gender, and sexuality). Because racial literacy is intrinsically intersectional, these other demographic identifiers can serve as a gateway to more direct reflections on race.

Additionally, you may want to make thematic connections between racial identity and the focus of the course you are teaching. In a media or film studies class, you might ask students if the characters they see in movies or on television look like them. In a history course, ask students to look back at the histories of the ethnic, racial, or other cultural groups with which they identify.

- **Is this a one-time assignment, or will students continue to revisit and revise it throughout the semester?** It is likely that students' perspectives of their own identities will change as they gather new understandings of race over the course of the semester. For this reason, it might be a good idea to have students return to the autobiographies to contextualize their earlier thoughts in scholarship and to reflect on any shifts (or lack thereof) in their ideas about identity. If you do require students to come back to the paper, consider turning it into a graded assignment. In addition to keeping the workload manageable (students might be frustrated working on an ungraded assignment multiple times in addition to their graded work), this approach helps students both see writing as a process and connect the personal with the academic.
- **Will students share these stories?** For many students, sharing personal stories can be intimidating, especially early in the semester when they don't know one another well. If they know others will be reading their work, they might also be more likely to hold back or temper their writing in order to present a particular persona to their audience. If you think this will be the case in your classroom, it might be a good idea to allow students to share the paper only with you. On the other hand, by sharing stories, students begin to see some of the more emotionalized and experiential aspects of race and identity, particular those of peers whose backgrounds differ from their own. Such glimpses into other perspectives can be transformative in the racial literacy classroom.

Whatever you decide, make the requirements clear to the students from the start. Not only will this prepare students for the assignment, but it also will encourage them to consider questions of audience as they craft their papers.

The racial autobiography is best assigned early in the semester and serves multiple functions for both teacher and student. For the teacher, it establishes a baseline of racial awareness for each student; teachers can then shape the rest of the curriculum to respond to the needs of the students in the classroom. The autobiography also allows instructors to assess their students' capabilities and tendencies with regards to essay writing.

Many composition programs mandate the assignment of a *diagnostic essay* in the first week of class to help instructors assess students' preexisting writing skills and areas that need improvement. For the racial literacy instructor—and anyone who might be uncomfortable with the pathological connotations that accompany the word *diagnostic*—the racial autobiography is a suitable replacement.

For students, the racial autobiography invites reflection without the pressure of direct interpersonal interaction. While much of the racial literacy curriculum requires such face-to-face dialogue, questions of race and identity can be intimidating for students, especially in the first weeks of the semester. By encouraging students to begin reflecting on their experiences with race from the privacy of their own notebooks or computers, students safely embark on a journey toward understanding their own positionality with regards to race and racism; this journey continues with the use of reflective essays and positionality maps.

Once students get to know one another inside the classroom, instructors may consider inviting students to share their personal narratives in small groups. The embodied learning that occurs when students share with and listen to one another can be transformative in understanding others' experiences and perspectives. Furthermore, by voicing their stories in front of a live audience rather than an invisible reader, students are encouraged to begin thinking about rhetorical elements like author and reader.

THE RACIAL AUTOBIOGRAPHY AT WORK: STUDENT VOICES

"The unconscious and invisible fact of my race and ethnicity never really played a defined role within my life. I cannot recall any instance where I was racially profiled, or taken advantage of due to my race or religion. However, I know that such a problem is real, and such a problem needs to be changed. . . . I have never really put much thought into the matter until I was asked to write this paper."

—Sam (White, Jewish, American)

"How do I write about race and racism without writing about all the negative things I've experienced? I don't want to turn this into a list of traumas."

—Andre (African American)

"In one of the towns that I lived in, I definitely dealt with feeling discriminated—I was constantly called the 'white' kid. A lot of my classmates in this town judged me based on the way I look, not even knowing my ethnicity was Puerto Rican."

—Jordan (Puerto Rican)

For some students, writing the racial autobiography will be the first time they have had to consider questions of individual racial identity. Other students may be frustrated that they are being asked to rehash painful experiences with racism.

In the first excerpt here, Sam expresses interest in exploring the systemic and symbolic functions of race but admits that he has never thought about his own racialized identity. He claims that, to his knowledge, no one has discriminated against him because of his race, but he does not acknowledge that his race itself has protected him from discrimination. Rather than identifying the presence of his Whiteness as a marker of social status, he identifies only the absence of discrimination, sidestepping any mention of their correlation. Sam seems to see race as somehow outside his lived experience.

That Sam conceives of racism as unrelated to his life as a White person is unsurprising, given that he had spent most of his life in predominantly White settings where the "very nature depends upon people *not* cultivating racial literacy."[11] In fact, racial literacy research has shown that students of *all* races struggle with the more personal aspects of racial identification; students generally have less trouble seeing that racial identities are learned than realizing that "*their* racial identities are learned too."[12] It is for this reason that the racial autobiography is so significant; not only does this initial exploration begin Sam's process of self-reflection, but it also helps both Sam and his instructor design a plan for his racial literacy work throughout the rest of the semester. From here, Sam's work will be in moving away from racial literacy as an intellectual endeavor and toward an embodied, experiential understanding of his own role as a racialized person within a larger racist society.

Unlike Sam, Andre appears to have thought about his experiences with racism and racialism. However, he, too, is hesitant to address these experiences in writing, though for different reasons. For Andre, recalling experiences with racism threatens to bring up painful feelings. Moreover, it appears he is also concerned about how his audience will perceive his writing, which he sees as a "list of traumas."

Students who have been subjected to racism may be uncomfortable rehashing painful experiences or feel annoyed that they have been asked to go over something they may already have spent time thinking about. It may be helpful to encourage students like Andre to approach the self-reflective aspect of the racial literacy curriculum with a more critical lens; inviting students to consider how their experiences are representative of larger societal problems and ideologies is an important component of the practice of racial literacy. Moreover, by asking students to look at the bigger picture, so to speak, they begin to consider more deeply the rhetorical significance of their narratives for an imagined audience. This awareness is an integral component of critical writing.

In the third excerpt, Jordan points to a significant problem of racialism (the assignment of racial identities as a system of classification): The use of skin color to categorize people overlooks a great deal of individual cultural identity. When others label Jordan based on his light skin, they ignore the ethnic identity with which he identifies most closely. While Whiteness confers privilege, being seen as White can also be reductive. Because appearance is one way in which individuals express their cultural identities, being seen as an outsider can harm one's sense of belonging.

Moreover, for an individual like Jordan who identifies as part of a minoritized group, the assignment of a White identity publicly denies that individual his experiences and feelings—positive or negative—as a minoritized individual. The assignment of traditionally sanctioned race labels like Black and White can prove particularly frustrating for biracial and multiracial individuals, who may feel they do not belong entirely with any racially identified group. For students like Jordan, the racial autobiography provides the opportunity to write a counternarrative to traditional racial discourse, using their personal stories to address larger political ideologies. In doing so, students begin to see that, by challenging misinformation and telling stories that are less frequently shared, they are not only reflecting on their experiences but also contributing their voices to a larger academic conversation.

INDIVIDUAL IDENTITY AND SOCIAL POSITIONALITY

After collecting racial autobiographies, instructors may find that individual students differ quite dramatically in their understandings of themselves as racialized beings. While students like Andre and Jordan may be aware of how the process of racialization has affected them, other students may understand themselves as raced by virtue of their skin color but be unsure how that identification influences their lived experiences. Students like Sam may even have difficulty identifying the factors that have contributed to their understandings of race and racism. Still other students may hold steadfastly to an idea of themselves as unique individuals; they may express the desire to identify as "human" or "just me." For this reason, it is important to remember that individual self-identity and social positionality are two very different entities.

Consider, for example, that Whiteness is an ambiguous concept with a "history of multiplicity."[13] Centuries ago, there were thought to be multiple White races; only in the twentieth century did anthropologists develop a theory of race that limited identity to White, Black, or Asian. At this point, ethnic groups that had previously been subjected to discrimination and violence in the United States, including the Irish, Italians, and Eastern European Jews, were absorbed into the umbrella categorization of Whiteness, despite their history of oppression. Moreover, despite this absorption, discrimination against these groups may persist. Given this history, it makes sense that an individual whose ancestors fled the country of their birth only to face more discrimination in the United States would identify foremost ethnically rather than by the racial categorization determined by the color of her skin.

However, while it is reasonable to get frustrated with the limitations of American racial classification, people must also admit that, regardless of individual ethnic heritage, American society continues to function within a racial binary. Therefore, ignoring one's perceived Whiteness is tantamount to embracing the privilege that skin color affords the individual.

A person who self-identifies as a White, Eastern European Jewish American may primarily be *identified* as White. The privilege one receives in a White hegemonic society has little to do with self-identification but everything to do with how he or she is identified by others. Acknowledging this distinction between self-identification and social categorization is integral to understanding American racialization and practicing racial literacy.

Instructional Strategy: Positionality Cluster Maps

To help students who are unsure of the many factors that contribute to the ways in which they view the world, teachers can use the positionality cluster map in figure 6.1. The positionality cluster map provides a tangible illustration of the rather abstract forces that contribute to an individual's experiences and understanding of the world. Some might think that breaking down individual and cultural identities into such tangible terms is reductive and dispassionate—and they would not be entirely wrong. After all, demographic classifications are not the only factors that make people who they are. However, because people tend to think more holistically about identity, this concrete map can help students break down that holistic social identity into specific, identifiable components. Concrete examples also help students better understand concepts that might otherwise seem theoretical, such as intersectionality. It is one thing to tell students that their identities are intersectional; it is another for

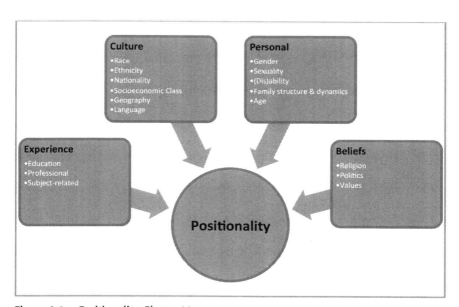

Figure 6.1. Positionality Cluster Map

them to see—in a visual representation—that they can identify simultaneously as Black, female, and middle class, for example.

The positionality cluster map, therefore, does not serve to teach students about their own identities—reflective writing like the racial autobiography is far more conducive to that purpose—but instead aims to point out the myriad spheres of influence that contribute to one's social positionality. That said, after students complete the maps, it is advisable to invite them to reflect (in freewriting, class discussion, or homework) on *how* those factors might contribute to their experiences and understandings of the world.

BUILDING THE BRIDGE: POSITIONALITY AS A KEY COMPONENT OF COMPOSITION

The sharing of personal experience is an opportunity for students to begin to consider their own positionality in relation to the broader social and cultural issues discussed in the racial literacy classroom. This dual reflection on the self as both an individual and a social being situated in the larger structures of society is key to uncovering the layered dimensions of race, racialism, and racism—and therefore one of the most significant components of racial literacy.

Personal writing allows students to identify the biases they may unconsciously possess that influence what they assume to be true about the world. By making tangible on the page what may otherwise remain uninvestigated, students begin to explore the situatedness of their own identities. The recognition of that situatedness helps students identify not only the deeply situated roles of race and racism but also the construction of experience, narrative, and text. Through the construction and telling of their own narratives, as well as through listening to others' stories, students begin to develop an awareness of the constructedness of text and the many factors that contribute to the effectiveness of a piece of writing. Put another way, telling their own stories invites students to explore the craft of storytelling itself.

How, then, can instructors help students use the self-reflective capacities they develop through racial literacy to better understand the concepts integral to composition studies and improve their writing skills?

Situating the Self and Appealing to Audience

One of the hardest skills for even the most experienced writers to master is how to convey their ideas to readers who may have vastly different experiences, beliefs, and understandings of the immediate material and the world in general. Memoir writing requires that one not only reflect on personal experience but also consider how those individual experiences resonate with an audience.

When students in the racial literacy classroom think about their experiences, they must also reflect on the social and cultural contexts that give that experience meaning. An experience is only meaningful because its surrounding contexts make it so. We experience the world through a series of imposed cultural identities—we are children, parents, lovers, students, artists, athletes—and meaning is ascribed through the ways in which we enact those roles. The same is true of how we tell and perceive the written narrative. For example, much of the significance of *A Child Called It*, Dave Pelzer's best-selling account of the abuse he suffered as a child, stems not only from the truth of the abuse but also from its perpetrator: The sadistic, alcoholic mother figure offends our cultural understanding of what it means to be a mother. Similarly, immigration stories are especially poignant during times of isolationist policy and anti-immigrant sentiment.

When Andre expressed concern in his racial autobiography that he was merely listing a series of traumatic experiences, he seemed to be concerned not only that he would have to dredge up those memories but also that he would be providing a reader a negative aesthetic experience with the text. The latter worry is actually an important indicator of Andre's understanding of the text as a transaction between the writer and the reader; because the reader gives meaning to a text as she makes meaning of it, the story ceases to exist without the reader's contribution in transforming it from "inkspots on paper" into "meaningful symbols."[14] While this perspective may be common among teachers and English education scholars, students often have trouble letting go of the *truth* of a true story.

Instructors who have taught personal narrative have likely engaged in some iteration of the following dialogue:

TEACHER: Why did you include this detail?

STUDENT: Because that's how it happened.

It is important to convey to students that the true story a writer tells in memoir is not a mere record of *what happened*. It is a *representation* of truth, crafted in the way that best conveys that truth to a particular audience. If we think of memoir as only the telling of experience, we reduce the craft and conventions of the genre to mere presentation (see figure 6.2). In memoir, the author must return to the story as he or she initiates the process of creation; the writer must re-create the story to represent that story.

Student writers must come to understand that "language and speech do not mirror experience; rather, they create representations of experience."[15] In the prewriting of memoir, writers identify the essence, so to speak, of the story: What is it about this particular story that demands to be told? What is the significance for the writer? What is the potential significance for the reader? What sort of aesthetic experience does the author want a reader to have?

In autobiography, there is often intrinsic interest in the subject of the work. Autobiographies tend to tell the life histories of celebrities, political figures, and others with established fame or notoriety. Employing the terminology of rhetorical case-study research, we might say that, rather than being of intrinsic interest, the

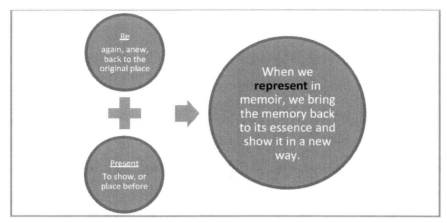

Figure 6.2. Memoir Writing as Representation

subject in memoir is a purposefully selected case that is representative of a particular phenomenon or experience. In other words, in order for memoir to be meaningful to the reader, the subject has to be made real through the telling of the narrative. Because the writer of memoir is also the subject of the story, individuals effectively re-create the self as they tell the story.

While writers must respect the conventions of the memoir genre (most importantly, that the story is true and being shared by a real person who experienced it), student writers must learn that the moment the writer becomes the narrator on the page, the self that is shared with the audience is an authorial construct. Through literary devices and rhetorical techniques, the writer performs a version of the self to be shared with the audience. Because identity is always plural and multidimensional, there is no single underlying self to which the narrative self of the memoir can be reduced. Instead there are layers of identity, imposed by society, interaction, expectation, and memory, that are peeled away or piled on to best represent the self of the author's choice to a given audience. The writer chooses what to share and how to share it based on both the experience and what the writer imagines an audience will deem significant.

Exploring positionality in a structured way before endeavoring to write memoir or personal narrative can help the student writer see that the narrative persona is not the real presentation of a true story but the representation of a life experience assigned significance by the sociocultural contexts in which it is situated, constructed by a writer who is simultaneously participant, observer, and storyteller.

Authorial Voice

Authorial voice is a unique persona and style created by an individual's combination of diction, syntax, arrangement, and other rhetorical and literary devices.

This nebulous concept is understood more easily through examples and experience: Consider the distinct authorial voices of Ernest Hemingway or William Faulkner. Hemingway was known for employing short sentences and direct, active verbs in what critics have long referred to as a masculine style of prose. Faulkner, on the other hand, wrote long and winding sentences heavy with stream-of-consciousness prose and sensory imagery.

While we tend to think of "voice" as belonging to the so-called creative writer, academic texts are in fact rich with authorial voice. For example, an engineering student writing a lab report must approximate the language and authority of an engineer. She must employ the diction, style, and rhetorical strategies of the engineer in order to position herself as the author of the report and the authority on its findings. At the same time, however, no two engineers—even those with the same awareness of the discursive practices of the field—sound exactly alike.

Returning to a literary example, consider that Hemingway and Faulkner were, essentially, contemporaries—both were celebrated American authors of the mid-twentieth century; both eventually won Nobel prizes; both have been absorbed into the modern literary canon; yet, interestingly, each has been quoted as decrying the other's authorial voice. More, then, must contribute to authorial voice than matters of place and time.

Place, of course, does contribute to an individual's diction and syntax. Words that identify even the most ordinary of concepts or items differ in different regions of the same country: the New Yorker might drive on a *parkway*, while his Californian friend commutes to work via *freeway*. The New Englander who enjoys a cold *soda* consumes the same beverage as her midwestern friend who drinks *pop*. The grammar and arrangement of words in a sentence are also geographically influenced: a southerner giving directions might advise a tourist to "go five mile up the road," a statement the northerner might deem grammatically incorrect because of the missing plural *s*.

Many of these regional differences stem from the linguistic differences of the peoples who reside in each part of the country. The omission of the letter *r* that is so distinctive of the New England dialect stems from the speech patterns of the early East Anglian Puritans who settled the region. The tendency for New Yorkers to transform the *th* sound into a *d*—turning *that*, *them*, and *those* into *dat*, *dem*, and *dose*—results from the area's settlement by the Dutch, whose language lacks interdental sounds like *th*. Later, the large Eastern European and Sephardic Jewish populations that settled New York City in the late nineteenth century contributed not only words and phrases to the New York lexicon—*chutzpah*, *shmuck*, *Get lost*—but also the identifiable prosody to New York dialect. Even the overlapping speech of New York English—which frustrated non–New Yorkers might refer to as "interrupting"— has been shown to be a convention with Yiddish influence.

African American vernacular English (AAVE, also referred to as African American English, Black English, or Black vernacular English) is influenced both by African language patterns and dialectical features of the southern United States. The omission of the copular conjugation of _to be_ in present tense—_He at work_; _She a writer_—and the use of the habitual _be_—_He been at work_; _She be writin' every day_—are thought to be derived from the syntactical structure of West African languages. The omission of the _g_ sound in the present progressive tense is similar to southern American English, as is the use of double negatives—_ain't, it don't mean nothing_—which was also a common feature of early English.

AAVE's influence has long extended beyond African American communities. The history of American slavery and the rearing of White children by African American slaves led to similarities between AAVE and the dialects spoken by southern Whites, particularly those of aristocratic lineages. Today, even the neophyte hip-hop fan likely knows that hip-hop and rap music have roots in the African American oral tradition. The popularity of hip-hop among contemporary youth, regardless of race, has also contributed to the use of AAVE among some White populations, particularly in urban areas.

Culture influences written and academic language practices, as well as oral communication. Because social and cultural conventions dictate the manner in which a story is told, two academic essay writers adhering to the same assignment guidelines might employ quite different modes of argumentation. Modes of argumentation and communication rooted in the African American oral tradition, such as signifying and narrative storytelling, might conflict with the expectations for critical writing in many classrooms, where standards of literacy stem from White European norms and values. Asian students might find that the modes of rhetoric employed in their communities differ from Western academic expectations. While Western rhetoric celebrates eloquence in writing and speech, Chinese rhetoric, for example, considers linguistic elegance a sign of pretense and disingenuousness.

Students raised with these cultural influences might approach writing assignments with ideas about effective argumentation that do not match their classmates'—or their teachers'—standards for success. For this reason, it is especially important that assignment guidelines are made clear to students and do not assume a shared cultural understanding, that guidelines are explained within the context of the course and the larger discursive norms of the academy and the field for which students are writing, and that teachers read and evaluate written work with an inclusive gaze.

Some features of voice are influenced by academic or professional rather than ethnic or geographic communities. The writer may use the term _workshop_ as a verb to mean sharing and critiquing written work, whereas the carpenter uses the same word as a noun to refer to a place. Studies have shown that scholars—in all fields of inquiry—tend to use longer sentences and more run-on sentences than those outside of the academy. Finally, some features of authorial voice are, of course, individual and subject to the same variations in personal taste as are food preference and style of dress. However, a thorough analysis of one's individual authorial voice necessitates a reflection on how even those seemingly individual preferences influence one's approach to communication and critical writing.

By mapping their regional, ethnic, and linguistic influences, students using the positionality cluster map begin to see how and from where their individual voices might have developed. As such, students begin to see that writing effectively is more than a matter of giving the teacher what she wants—a strategy that, in the quest for academic success, is often deemed the path of least resistance. Instead, students in the racial literacy classroom are guided toward an understanding that successful written communication originates from the author's evaluation of both self and audience and the careful selection of appropriate linguistic and rhetorical bridges to connect writer and reader.

Text as Construct

Rather than encouraging a holistic approach to questions of social identity, the positionality cluster map asks students instead to delineate the specific factors that together make up their identities—by breaking down these components, students move through the processes of analysis that too often are sacrificed as they eagerly jump to more-conclusive interpretations. In addition to encouraging students to see their own writing from a craft-based perspective, instructors can also use the positionality cluster map to draw parallels between self-reflection and textual analysis.

When students attempt to analyze texts, they often jump directly to their interpretations. Getting students to articulate the textual data they have synthesized and the cognitive processes they have taken to get to that interpretation can be a challenge for even the most process-oriented instructor. These steps, however, are integral to students' developing metacognitive awareness: How have they come to their conclusions? What did they know before? What do they know now? And, more importantly, what steps did they take to get from one point to the next?

In textual analysis, this process often involves identifying significant words or phrases in a text, drawing connections between those words or phrases and other words or phrases in the texts, adding extratextual information to provide context as necessary, and synthesizing distinct pieces of literary "data" (such as literacy devices and techniques) to come to a broader interpretation. While for some students this is a seemingly automatic process—if the student is asked how he has come to an interpretation, he might respond "I can just tell"—learning to articulate each step is integral to developing an understanding of text as construct.

This is even more important when the student shifts roles from reader to writer. In order to craft a successful academic essay, the student must identify the best way to break down an idea in order to convey it to an audience. When highly experientially informed subjects like racism are introduced, however, strong emotional reactions can lead individuals to jump to conclusions or respond with overall impressions rather than thoroughly articulating the key reasoning behind their arguments or the steps they have taken to reach those conclusions. The positionality cluster map can be used to help students practice breaking down ideas into smaller, articulable parts.

The awareness needed to convey an argument is actually quite similar to one of the foundational elements of teaching. Even when we know something, whether because of belief, experience, or education, in order to teach it, we must imagine *unknowing* it. Only then can we determine the best approaches by which we can convey this information to others. Given this parallel to teaching, instructors might encourage students to walk their peers, step by step, through their own thinking processes around racially charged issues—to *teach* their classmates how they have arrived at their conclusions. This approach aligns with educational models of apprenticeship, "flipping" the classroom, and activity theory.

Moving Outward from the Personal

By looking at themselves as texts, students also consider the ways in which individual experiences are representative of larger social truths. In the racial literacy classroom, this is an especially important step in helping students to move past understanding racism as individual acts of discrimination to examine fully the cultural ideologies and institutional systems that maintain racial inequity. Moving outward from the personal also enables students to consider the role of the personal in academic discourse.

Many students are warned to avoid the use of first person in academic writing. While this is true for some fields of study, especially in the natural sciences, in many fields the writer—as research instrument and interpreter—is present in the text. By scaffolding writing assignments from the internal (personal narrative) to the external (research-based), instructors can introduce discussion around the discourse-specific use of the narrative self in academic writing.

For example, the biologist employs third person and passive voice in her lab report to emphasize the experiment rather than the researcher and ensure readers of its replicability. (In short, if the right steps are employed, any biologist ought to reach the same conclusions.) A team of ethnographers, on the other hand, who have spent sixteen months living among and studying a particular group of people, will necessarily include their own observations and impressions. The ethnographers who both observe and participate are intrinsically part of the research because their own positionalities influence which information they have gathered, how study participants have responded to them, and how they interpret their findings. Ensuring replicability in this case is less important than demonstrating validity by convincing readers that the research was soundly conducted and that its findings are logical and well-supported by data collection.

Even academic writing that employs first-person narrative is not solely *about* the individual—it is about the individual as representative. Drawing connections between one's personal experiences and other individuals' experiences also enables the student writer to "pluralize," generalize, and effectively move away from purely personal narratives toward the content and style of academic writing.[16]

This is especially significant when students are writing research-based papers, as is increasingly the case in the critical writing classroom. How do we draw conclusions from individual experiences, narratives, and case studies? The research writer must extrapolate from available data to examine whether individual experience is generalizable or representative of a larger truth. Generalizations present the racial literacy educator with a paradox of sorts; we are taught to avoid stereotypes and essentialism, yet the nature of academic communication demands some generalization.

The conclusion section of a research paper does far more than restate the introduction or key points of the paper; it instead looks to the future, considering the implications of the research presented. Instead of asking "What did you learn?" the implications section of a research paper asks students to consider not only what they have learned but also why it is important and what can be done with the new information. In the racial literacy classroom, this future-oriented gaze is especially important, as it offers students a sense of hope and determination in the face of societal problems that often seem insurmountable.

When suggesting the implications of research, one may consider how a study's findings might be considered or applied by individuals, groups, and larger systems or institutions. An individual reviewing the research might wonder how to apply its findings directly to his or her life; a group of scholars might find suggestions for how to undertake future related research; and policy makers or administrators might come upon suggestions for structural changes that could be made, taking into account the study's major findings. These three levels of implications directly parallel the three levels on which racial literacy considers race and racism: the psychological or personal, the interpersonal, and the systemic.[17] Let's take a look at an example in table 6.2.

While the five-paragraph essay remains a staple of secondary writing instruction and standardized testing, many instructors lament students' reliance on its reductive formula. Teachers frustrated by the simplicity of the five-paragraph essay model may prefer to frame writing assignments, particularly research-based papers, around the format of a scholarly research report. The scholarly research paper invites students to explore the many ways data—experiential, textual, or statistical—may be interpreted and presented and encourages a deeper exploration of what it means to write for an academic audience.

CONCLUDING THOUGHTS

Scaffolding writing assignments in the racial literacy classroom from the personal to the academic is a practical and emotionally sensitive way to introduce students to writing about race. Not only does the practice of reflective writing encourage students to see how they themselves fit into larger questions about race and racism, but also beginning with what they know from experience eases students into conversations and debates that can otherwise seem abstract and difficult to articulate. The

Table 6.2. Three Levels of Research Implications

A group of student researchers have informally observed that few students in their academic cohort dine regularly in the school cafeteria. Armed with the overarching research question "What are students' attitudes toward this university's cafeteria?" they interview a representative sample of their peers, and once they have gathered some preliminary data, they distribute a survey to the entire student body. The major findings are as follows:

1. Students believe that cold food in the school cafeteria (sandwiches, prepackaged items) is overpriced and prefer to buy similar items at local convenience stores.
2. Students who commute to campus and do not live in the residence halls bring food from home.
3. Students with dietary restrictions (vegetarian, vegan, kosher, gluten free) believe that the school cafeteria lacks adequate options to suit their diets.

What are the study's implications?

Psychological level (individuals)	• Students who currently dine in the cafeteria might consider shopping at local stores or bringing food from home instead. • Students who do not dine in the cafeteria might consider purchasing more affordable hot items in the cafeteria rather than cold items.
Interpersonal level (small groups)	• Researchers ought to conduct research in other local universities to determine whether these findings are campus-specific or indicative of a larger problem related to university dining. • Student groups like student government and cultural clubs could petition the university for more inclusive menu options.
Systemic level (larger groups and institutions)	• University administration must introduce a more inclusive food menu that addresses the dietary needs of all members of the student body. • The university should conduct an audit of school cafeteria finances to determine where cuts might be made to reduce prices of cold items.

eventual transition from personal writing to academic and research-based papers can help teachers begin to explore with their students rhetorical concepts like author, audience, genre, disciplinarity, and representation.

Most importantly, personal writing invites students to consider how lived experiences with race, racism, and racialism—including but not limited to their own—can contribute to a broader academic understanding of societal inequity. If there is one tenet that must be conveyed to students in the racial literacy classroom, it is this: Their experiences are *real*—and they *matter*.

NOTES

1. Norman K. Denzin, *Interpretive Autoethnography* (Los Angeles: Sage, 2014), 32.

2. Sue William Silverman, preface to *Fearless Confessions: A Writer's Guide to Memoir* (Athens: University of Georgia Press, 2009).

3. David Takacs, "How Does Your Positionality Bias Your Epistemology?" *Thought and Action* (2003): 29.

4. Allison Skerrett, Alina Adonyi Pruitt, and Amber S. Warrington, "Racial and Related Forms of Specialist Knowledge on English Education Blogs," *English Education* 47, no. 4 (2015): 319.

5. Michael Omi and Howard Winant, *Racial Formation in the United States: From the 1960s to the 1990s* (New York: Routledge, 1994), 71–72.

6. Lee Gutkind, *Keep It Real: Everything You Need to Know about Researching and Writing Creative Nonfiction* (New York: Norton, 2008), 98.

7. Yolanda Sealey-Ruiz, "From Writing for Full Presence to 'Where I'm From': Writing That Builds Community in the Classroom," *Hip-Hop in the Heartland Annual Teacher Summer Institute* (Madison, WI, 2015).

8. For more on "Breathing to Write," see Mara Lee Grayson, "Breathing to Write: Moments of Yoga in First Year Composition," *Teaching English in the Two-Year College* 44, no. 4 (2017): 450–52; and chapter 5 of this book.

9. See Gita DasBender, "Critical Thinking in College Writing: From the Personal to the Academic," in *Writing Spaces: Readings on Writing*, vol. 2, eds. Charles Lowe and Pavel Zemliansky (West Lafayette, IN: Parlor Press, 2011); and Janet Emig, "Writing as a Mode of Learning," *College Composition and Communication* 28, no. 2 (1977): 122–28.

10. For more on the use of literacy narratives, see Margaret Byrd Boegeman, "Lives and Literacy: Autobiography in Freshman Composition," *College English* (1980): 662–69; and Christina Ortmeier-Hooper, "English May Be My Second Language, but I'm Not 'ESL,'" *College Composition and Communication* (2008): 389–419.

11. Amy E. Winans, "Cultivating Racial Literacy in White, Segregated Settings: Emotions as Site of Ethical Engagement and Inquiry," *Curriculum Inquiry* 40, no. 3 (2010): 476.

12. Amy Vetter and Hannah Hungerford-Kressor, "'We Gotta Change First': Racial Literacy in a High School English Classroom," *Journal of Language and Literacy Education* 10, no. 1 (2014): 92.

13. Nell Irvin Painter, "What Is Whiteness?" *New York Times*, June 21, 2015, 8.

14. Louise M. Rosenblatt, *Literature as Exploration*, 5th ed. (New York: Modern Language Association of America, 1995), 21.

15. Denzin, *Interpretive Autoethnography*, 37.

16. James Moffett, "Bridges: From Personal Writing to the Formal Essay," *Center for the Study of Writing* (March 1989): 7.

17. Lani Guinier, "From Racial Liberalism to Racial Literacy: *Brown v. Board of Education* and the Interest-Divergence Dilemma," *Journal of American History* 91, no. 1 (2004): 115.

7

Controversial Conversations

What We (Don't) Say

> "Figuring out how race matters thus involves attention not just to moments when we talk overly easily 'about race,' but also to moments when we resist talking about race at all."

> —Mica Pollock[1]

One of the most important characteristics of racial literacy is the development of discursive practices with which to talk about race and racism. This is necessary not only because of how prevalent racism is in our society but also because of how difficult it is to talk about race. Many individuals, including those with supposedly progressive ideals of equity and social justice, were raised *not* to talk about race—or other controversial subjects, such as religion and politics—in public spaces among those who may not share their beliefs.

Some individuals avoid these conversations out of fear of offending those around them. Others want to talk but aren't sure how to go about it, where to begin, or what language to use. Sometimes race talk isn't explicit but implied through language that dances around race, whether that covertness is intentional or not. In these situations, what is unsaid is just as important as what *is* said, if not more. What people don't say can be hidden by what they *do* say—and without paying careful attention to subtext, silences, and substitutions, individuals may perpetuate problematic discourses even when they seem to be critiquing those same discourses.

There are two types of silence likely to occur in the racial literacy classroom. The first is not exclusive to the racial literacy curriculum, but it is easy to identify and poses the most immediate practical obstacle for instructors: Students aren't talking. As any experienced instructor likely knows, when a number of students aren't vocally participating in the classroom, it is hard to keep conversation going. In this case, students who do talk feel that the burden to maintain dialogue has been placed on their shoulders, a responsibility that is not only frustrating but can also distract from some of the more important work of the curriculum. Silence can even seem to be contagious—students who are hesitant to speak in class to begin with may feel little incentive to make the effort once it is obvious that their classmates are not doing the same. For the teacher, too, silence can be overwhelming. Instructors may be forced to lecture longer than intended or to fill time with unplanned activities. They may feel that they are not getting through to their students or that they have failed to implement the curriculum.

The second type of silence is more insidious and can be harder to identify. The hidden silence of racial discourse emerges in classroom conversation or in student writing and even when students are active participants in the curriculum—but when much is still left unsaid. Students might talk about everything but race. They might talk about a particular racial group but not another. They might substitute polite, inaccurate language for terms that are more applicable but that make them uncomfortable. They might misuse terminology or employ racialized language without meaning to do so. Sometimes this silence is intentional; other times students may not even be aware of this silence.

This chapter first addresses the more practical silence of the classroom, as it is often easier to identify, if not remedy, before delving into the ideological silences that undergird racial discourse—and that must be examined for students to think critically about the roles of language and rhetoric in racial hierarchy and systemic oppression.

SILENCE IN THE CLASSROOM

"Are we . . . allowed . . . to talk about this stuff?"

—Chloe (White)

While many scholars contend that race talk should be encouraged in the academic environment, not all students are comfortable with such conversations. A number of reasons may factor into a student's decision to remain silent, from the ideological, including cultural norms or unwillingness to share unpopular opinions, to the personal and practical, such as individual fatigue or disinterest.

Cultural Norms and Marginalized Voices

Many scholars have observed that students of Asian descent tend to be less vocal in the classroom than their non-Asian classmates. English classrooms today tend to operate within the conventions of the Western conversation model, which encourages assertive verbal contribution. This can be particularly difficult for Asian and Asian American students, as Asian cultural values largely stress "indirectness, subtlety, and cooperation in interacting with others."[2]

Even more problematic is that students are often graded in part on these cultural norms. Participation, as most often defined by contributions to class discussion, is frequently listed as a criterion for assessment in the college classroom. While participation is a requisite of the racial literacy curriculum, instructors ought to amend their syllabi to list the different types of participation that are considered acceptable, including attendance, presence in online discussion boards, and active listening, in order to include students who are uncomfortable speaking in class for personal or cultural reasons.

Students of color may be less vocal in the classroom for another reason. The racial literacy classroom is, by nature, critical—yet classrooms tend to operate within White Eurocentric norms. The liberal arts curriculum is derived from ancient Greek and Enlightenment era beliefs about knowledge and civic participation. The systems of grading imply a belief in meritocracy. Positions of power and policy continue to be held predominantly by White administrators.

Even in the racial literacy classroom, it is impossible to escape the influence of racial inequity on educational practices and policies. Students of color may fear the consequences of speaking out against an ethnocentric White European system, especially in an educational institution itself built from a White European model. This is important for instructors to acknowledge—both as they plan the racial literacy curriculum and as they communicate with their students.

On the contrary, some educators have found that students of color are the most vocal when in-class conversation turns to matters of race and racism. Because racism most negatively affects the lives of people of color, students from historically oppressed and marginalized groups may have the most to say about racism, particularly from the experiential perspective. To some extent, this specialized knowledge invites students of color, who traditionally have had less voice in White European American educational institutions, to assume the role of expert in the classroom. Unfortunately, this also places a heavy burden on the students who are likely already most burdened by the effects of racism. Instructors must take care to ensure that traditionally underrepresented students have a voice in the classroom without also being given the responsibility of tending to their White classmates.

Political Correctness and White Fragility

While educational norms and the structure of the classroom may seem most suited to the White student population, in the racial literacy classroom, White individuals may be some of the most stubbornly silent students. For some White students, this silence is evidence of, at best, naïveté, or, at worst, willful blindness. White students who don't understand or who don't want to understand that race and racism affect everyone may see the racial literacy curriculum as irrelevant to their lives or academic careers.

The troubling part of this is that, to some extent, they may be right. In a society that values Whiteness, White students *can* get away with being unaware of their own positionality. The racial literacy curriculum, however, doesn't aim to help students simply get by. They must move forward with increased awareness of themselves, their peers, and the world outside of the classroom. As such, some White students may become more vocal as the semester progresses; as they better understand how race and racism influence their own lives, they are likely to be more regular contributors to classroom discussions.

Some White students actually want to talk about race but avoid speaking directly and honestly for fear of being viewed as racist. They may censor themselves even when they have legitimate questions about race and racism out of concern that those questions aren't "politically correct" or appropriate to ask.

Broadly, political correctness denotes the avoidance of potentially offensive language and the preference of culturally sensitive terminology and actions that are cognizant of the history of oppression and marginalization, with particular regard to race and gender. The term has long been linked to a connotation of excessive censorship. Moreover, the emphasis on the language used distracts both individuals and institutions from addressing the deeper sociopolitical effects of discrimination and oppression.

Because so much of the racial literacy curriculum is about openness and critical discourse, political correctness poses unique challenges for racial literacy instructors and their students. Students' awareness of political correctness functions on a spectrum. On one end, students like Chloe, who cautiously asked if she and her classmates were "allowed" to talk about racism, may acknowledge yet question the politically correct mores of racial discourse. On the other end, students may be as curious as Chloe but fear even asking the question. It is important not to allow this silence to go unchecked, thus being normalized in the racial literacy classroom.

Some scholars have noted that curricula aimed toward equity and the education of students of color inadvertently marginalize White students.[3] Some might argue that, given the historic and continued marginalization of students of color, this dynamic is a necessary turn. However, the racial literacy curriculum must address the influence of race and racism on society at large and consider the racialized experiences of all students, regardless of their ethnic or racial affiliation.

At the same time, it is not unlikely that the curriculum will be perceived by some White students—whose comfort has been maintained and supported by the status quo of academia—as discriminatory or favoring students of color. With a well-designed racial literacy curriculum in place, this perspective will not be permanent but instead a phase some students will pass through as they move along in the course. It is imperative, therefore, that instructors, even in predominantly White institutions, do not abandon this curriculum or amend its implementation to appease the denial-based reactions of White students.

This is especially important given that such trends may be occurring on a larger scale in academic institutions. In recent years, trigger warnings and safe spaces have gained popularity—and notoriety—on college campuses. Trigger warnings, statements spoken or written before texts and intended to alert readers to potentially emotionally disturbing material, may be introduced in the classroom when students are assigned to read texts that address subjects like rape, child abuse, war, and other traumatic experiences that could lead to retraumatization for individual readers. It is arguable that these warnings have increased in popularity largely due to increased awareness of problems like post-traumatic stress disorder, including among the military veteran population. Some educators find these warnings help students to better prepare themselves to read such material, while others find the practice infantilizing, arguing that part of education is the expansion of knowledge and the encountering of new information, even if it causes distress.

The term *safe space* likely originated from the women's movements of the 1970s but is most closely associated with LGBTQIA+ communities. In recent years, safe spaces, often outwardly identifiable by an inverted pink triangle, have served as a way for educators and others on school campuses to demonstrate that they are gay-rights allies and that they do not tolerate homophobic hate speech in their offices and related spaces. In this way, those spaces could be identified by gay students as safer than others on campus. More recently, the concept has been used to denote any space where students of a particular marginalized group can come together to speak freely about that marginalization without fear of reproach.

Some critics of safe spaces contend that they infringe on freedom of speech and that, by designating a space safe for some students, they are also silencing others. That these others tend to be White students has led some educators to deem this criticism racially motivated. Other educators argue that safe spaces prevent important conversations from happening across the university. When students only share with peers who share their experiences and beliefs, they lose the opportunity to learn from—and perhaps educate—those whose experiences differ from their own.

Trigger warnings and safe spaces might present another problem, particularly where spaces like the racial literacy classroom are concerned. While these measures may have been created to protect students who have experienced suffering and marginalization, by labeling certain texts and designating only certain spaces as safe, instructors and administrators continue to nudge these students and their stories to the margins of the university. In this way, trigger warnings and safe spaces ultimately serve not as protection for students of underrepresented populations or with traumatic experiences but as a cushion to protect the fragility of the predominantly White student population.

The racial literacy classroom cannot be designated a safe space in the way that the term has come to be understood in educational institutions. However, instructors must build for their students a safe space, to the extent that it is possible when a diverse group of individuals talk about potentially painful conversations (see box 7.1). While no specific subject matter should be labeled off-limits, part of racial literacy is learning how to talk about race, racism, and related matters. As demonstrated in chapter 5, students will have emotional reactions. The safety of the classroom lies in how those reactions are shared, addressed, and accepted.

BOX 7.1.   "I'M NOT UNCOMFORTABLE; I'M JUST SHY!"

Remember that there is a distinction between being silent and being silenced. Silence in the racial literacy classroom may actually have nothing to do with race talk. Students may avoid sharing because of interpersonal issues, such as a recent breakup or family dispute; physiological issues, like lack of sleep or a nervous stutter; or academic concerns unrelated to the racial literacy classroom, including difficulties completing an assignment or worry about a midterm exam scheduled later in the week. Such silences may be temporary. Consider that you, too, may be more hesitant to share with colleagues when you are feeling unwell or have a big presentation coming up.

When you notice that a student has been quiet in your classroom, make sure you consider what you know about the individual and the classroom context in which the silence occurred before jumping to the conclusion that the student is feeling uncomfortable. Consider the time of day and whether that student has missed class recently. Recall what that student has told you about his extracurricular activities or familial obligations. Finally, see what happens the next time the class meets. If the silence becomes a pattern and if after some time you believe something more is happening, gently inquire as to the situation privately after class. For a student who is feeling uneasy, a gentle reminder that you are listening may be all that is needed to ease the discomfort.

INSTRUCTIONAL STRATEGY: LEAD-DISCUSSANT GROUPS

Regardless of the reasons behind it, students' silence in the classroom can make it difficult to explore the racial literacy curriculum to its full extent. As such, instructors must find strategies that engage students in active participation without the pressure of cold-calling during class discussion or solo presentations.

How It Works

Each week the class meets, a pair or group of three students should lead the rest of the class in a discussion of or an activity related to the readings that were due that day. Students should self-nominate but should not choose their groupmates; instead they should sign up for a particular date based on that session's theme or the readings assigned for that week. Ideally, sign-up will occur on the first or second day of the semester so that students are informed of the activity and are given time to prepare themselves, intellectually and emotionally, to lead part of that class session.

Students should receive little direction for the assignment—part of the work is figuring out for themselves how to structure the session. It is important, however, that students are given any related readings at least two weeks in advance of their discussion date. While this may mean they have access to readings before the rest of their classmates, it ensures that they have adequate time to plan and alleviates some of the last-minute panic many students feel before an assignment deadline.

At thirty to forty-five minutes long, the lead-discussant activity is not likely to fill an entire class session. It is possible, however, that the conversations that are initiated by students acting as lead discussants *will* occupy the remainder of class time. As such, instructors should feel free to jump in at any point. If the class meets twice weekly, then it is advisable to only ask students to lead the discussion in one of those sessions. If the class meets once a week, a midclass break would be a good transition between the lead-discussant activity and the remainder of the class. If, however, the class meets three times a week for less than an hour, then it is fitting that one session each week be devoted to the lead-discussant activity and any class discussions that arise therefrom.

Regardless of how often the class meets, students should not be pressured to cover the entirety of that week's reading in discussion. Instead, the activity should in some way draw on that week's material. The activity should be grounded in the theoretical concepts presented in those readings or illuminate those ideas in a way that encourages deeper exploration of the material. Ideally, the activity will also encourage student participation, though there are a few different approaches that can be taken by students (and instructors; see box 7.2).

Finally, all students should submit a brief paper (one to two pages) describing the activity or presentation, why they chose to present the material this way, and how the activity relates to the theoretical concepts or skills of the racial literacy curriculum. Instructors may require this assignment be turned in on the day of the presentation, or they may choose to wait until after the activity to collect the papers. If they choose the latter, then students may also use the writing to reflect on their experiences with the activity, including how they felt leading the discussion, how their classmates responded, and any new insights they have gained about the material following the presentation.

Why It Works

> In his racial literacy classroom, Ricky, a male-identifying student with a high-pitched voice, made a comment with which many of his classmates agreed. One classmate, Joseph, raised his hand to add on, "I agree with what she said," pointing to Ricky, before continuing to comment. Ricky opened his mouth but quickly closed it. Ricky's instructor, in whom he had previously confided his identification as a transgender male, caught his eye, but Ricky quickly shook his head no. During the class's midsession fifteen-minute break, the instructor asked Ricky if he would like to address the issue after the break.
>
> "No," Ricky said. "I'll talk about it next week during my lead-discussant activity."

BOX 7.2.   THREE MODELS FOR LEAD DISCUSSANTS

Student as Presenter

This model emphasizes the leading role of the lead discussants. Students employing this approach will likely behave as teachers, standing before the classroom and walking their classmates through the material. This approach is most similar to a formal presentation. Students might create PowerPoint presentations to break down and explain difficult ideas. They might also incorporate brief viewings of related film or viral clips.

Student as Collaborator

In this model, the lead discussants work alongside their classmates to make sense of difficult passages or concepts in a particular text. Students may highlight sections they themselves are struggling with. This approach allows lead discussants to admit their own lack of expertise, which may ease some of the pressure of leading the discussion. Activities designed within this model include small-group discussions (in which lead discussants join individual groups) and whole-class conversations.

Student as Game Master

In the game master model, lead discussants guide their classmates through an activity meant to illuminate some part of the class material. Related activities may include surveys and questionnaires, which students can complete individually or in small work groups, problem-solving puzzles or scavenger hunts, or appropriate physical activities. Because this approach requires the most active class participation, be sure that your students run their ideas by you prior to conducting the activity.

The lead-discussant activity creates the opportunity for students to focus on material they believe to be significant. It also allows the instructor to see how students are making sense of the readings and working through their ideas about course content. Some students will call on their experiential knowledge as they develop lead-discussant activities, as was the case with Ricky, the student in the example shared here. Ricky had signed up to lead the class discussion on a day on which one of the main session topics would be intersectionality and the interplay between race and gender. From discussions he had had with his instructor, his instructor knew that these were subjects that mattered to Ricky. Ricky chose not to address a difficult situation that arose in the classroom because he knew he would have a more structured opportunity to do so the next week.

His instructor also demonstrated a keen sensitivity to the needs of the classroom at that moment. By catching Ricky's eye, the instructor deferred to the comfort of the student rather than the ideological concept that had suddenly presented itself. Comments that are offensive or inaccurate need to be addressed, but they do not necessarily need to be called out on the spot. In this situation, coming back to the problem later on allowed Ricky and his groupmates to consider the best way to approach the issue. The additional time also gave Ricky space to process the feelings that had likely arisen during the awkward classroom exchange. The lead-discussant activity gives students like Ricky the opportunity to act as experts in the classroom.

Other students may sign up to lead discussions on topics on which they don't consider themselves experts. The lead-discussant activity invites these students to dive more deeply into a field of inquiry that may until then appear elusive. Importantly, especially for quieter students or those who don't already feel like experts on the material, the lead-discussant activity provides a means for individuals to enter difficult conversations. Because students plan the activity together, they can workshop their ideas or practice presenting the activity before the actual assignment is due. For students who are shy or who fear saying the wrong thing in front of their peers, the support they receive from their lead-discussant groupmates may provide the encouragement needed to move outside their comfort zones.

PUBLIC DISCOURSE AND RACIAL INEQUITY

Political correctness may have changed the language of race in the public sphere, but has it changed the lived realities of racism? Despite increasing neoliberal claims of postracialism, shifts in racial discourse since the civil rights era have only reified, albeit in new ways, the existing racial order of White supremacy in American society. The strategic, intentional silences of political correctness play a significant sociopolitical role. Consider, for example, the recent use of coded language to describe White supremacist groups; even mainstream media have referred to these extremists as *alt-right*, a clever term that glosses over the groups' neo-Nazi ideologies.

In short, rewriting language around race has not served to reconfigure our longstanding racial hierarchy or improve opportunities for people of color. The framework of racial literacy demands that students learn to both talk about race in productive ways and critically analyze how race is talked about more publicly, especially when race doesn't appear to be part of the conversation at all.

Hidden Ideologies of Racial Discourse

During a discussion of the way the media had addressed recent incidences of police brutality against men of color, Mimi, who self-identified as blended, took issue

with the use of the term *Black* to identify people of African descent: "I don't even
like saying Black people. It's Brown—Black's not even a color. Is anybody really
Black? It's a label!"

Her classmates seemed to agree with the inappropriateness of *Black* as a race
label. Cora, who herself identified as Black, noted that no one really had black
skin. Amina, who had been born in Egypt and identified as Arabic, pointed out,
however, that "Brown is the same thing. It's just a different color."[4]

It is imperative that students decode and interrogate the language of race and racism. Sometimes, however, *how* those students critique racialized language can be as
problematic as the language itself. While Mimi's analysis of race labels demonstrates
her increasing awareness of racialized language, it also betrays the insidiousness of
racialism itself. Her frustration with the visual inaccuracy of *Black* as a racial identification and her stated preference of *Brown* seems an attempt to reconfigure race not
as a social construct but as a physical characteristic. While she seems to recognize
that these terms are labels, in moving from *Black* to *Brown*, she relies on a similar
pseudoscientific categorization of race as a biological trait. As Amina points out,
Mimi ultimately reifies rather than reconstructs race, merely renaming categories "to
create others that seem more appealing."[5]

Even more difficult to identify and deconstruct is the way race is coded into
seemingly innocuous language. When people do not directly address race, they talk
around it. Often, such evasive speech nonetheless makes clear that race is in fact
the topic of conversation. For example, an individual who has just moved to a new
city might be warned by a long-time resident to avoid certain "bad neighborhoods."
Because of the interplay between race and poverty in urban settings, so-called bad
neighborhoods are likely impoverished and non-White. Two people's mutual understanding of the existing racial hierarchy and covert racial discourse allows the listener
to infer the implication of the speaker's statement without either party ever having
to address race directly, let alone consider why the conflation of *non-White* and *bad*
is problematic.

Race is also coded into dialogue that, on the surface, does not even appear to be
about race. For example, *redneck*, a piece of language that does not immediately
seem to be associated with race at all, has historically been used by Whites to identify White people who behave "in ways supposedly unbecoming to or unexpected
of Whites."[6] More recently, some comedians and country musicians have used this
term to mockingly refer to themselves and their own experiences. A similar word,
ghetto, has evolved over time from its anti-Semitic roots in Europe to its euphemis-
tic reference to poor, Black communities in U.S. cities. It has also evolved from a
place-naming noun to a descriptive adjective. The term continues to be used both
in popular culture and in more formal communications, and many students refer to
people or places as *ghetto* without taking note of the way this piece of language may
serve to perpetuate racial inequity.

Intentional Silences: Equity and Word Choice

> Magdalena, a sociology professor and the director of her university's multicultural affairs office, hosted a dinner party. She invited some colleagues, including the new faculty advisor for the school's LGBTQIA+ club, as well as a few friends who worked outside of academia. Two of these guests were a gay couple who had recently married after more than two decades together. One was an attorney, the other a recently retired public-school social worker. Both had been long-time participants in gay rights activism. Upon meeting the new faculty advisor, the attorney confessed that he had no idea what the last two letters in the club's name represented.
>
> "*I* stands for *intersex*," said Magdalena, "and *A* is *asexual*. The plus sign—"
>
> "Plus sign?" the social worker interrupted. "There's a plus sign?"

As evidenced by the exchange between Magdalena and her friends, even some people who have been advocates for social equity are not up to date on the most appropriate academic terminology to describe their efforts or ideals. There is arguably a disjunction between the discourse of the academy and the lived experiences of individuals outside the academy. This disconnect applies to issues of race, as well as gender and sexuality. Complicating matters further, the language that is deemed most appropriate changes over time to incorporate new knowledge.

Individuals who have not had a strong education in sociology or social equity may not understand why certain measures have been implemented or why certain terminology around race, gender, and other demographics is preferable to other language practices. To these students—and some teachers—the regulation of language practices may instead feel like excessive political correctness or censorship.

Because that feeling may cause students to avoid sharing or asking questions, students in the racial literacy classroom must be allowed to use the wrong language—at first. They must then be informed, without accusation, as to why what they have said is deemed inappropriate or offensive. This can open a deeper discussion of how language reflects racial ideology. Rather than deeming certain language unsuitable, educators and students ought to interrogate the ideologies that underlie not only the words we say (or do not say) but also the ideologies and sociopolitical shifts that underlie the changes in language use over time.

TEACHER RESOURCE: THE WORD BIOGRAPHY

> "Like with the N-word. When Black people use it between them, fine. If White people use it, then I'm like, what are you talking about? No! Even if it's Black people, I'm like, what are they talking about? This means something. Our ancestors fought so hard against it, and now people are accepting it. If you call somebody a nigger—why would you want to be referred to as that? It makes the struggle not worth it."
>
> —Jezebel (African American)

"You're totally missing the point. It acknowledges the struggle."

—Chantel (African American)

Words have value. They have value because of the concepts to which they refer; because of their associations and connotations, as well as their dictionary denotations; and because of their histories. Language is dynamic, not static, and words and phrases often start off being used in one way and evolve over time to take on new meanings or are used in different ways.

The word biography paper asks students to look at the living history of a piece of language. Countless terms and phrases, many of which today seem benign and are used regularly in both colloquial speech and academic discourse, have racist histories, of which many individuals are unaware. By exploring where and when a word came into usage or prevalence and how the usage of that word has evolved over time, students learn both that language is not static and that language has served a key function in the maintenance of racial oppression.

Though students may not reach this question, let alone come to an answer, in their individual papers, the overarching point of inquiry here is whether language can truly change meaning or if its history dictates its future. Can language be reappropriated? This appears to be the deeper question guiding the debate that Jezebel and Chantel, the two students quoted at the beginning of this section, found themselves in their racial literacy classroom. Anyone who has had a similar conversation has likely discovered that the answer, if they manage to come to one, is never as simple as a "yes" or "no," and more often than not, the question becomes increasingly complex the more it is discussed. Perhaps, then, the debate itself is more important than the answer (or answers) one seeks.

Each student can be assigned a word, choose a word from a list provided by the instructor, or suggest a word or phrase to focus on in the essay. Box 7.3 lists some words and phrases that have racialized roots, so to speak. These terms have been used to refer pejoratively to racial groups, to stand in for more direct language about race, or to refer to places or things that were part of historical racism.

What is emphasized in this living history will differ based on the demands of the course. In First-Year Composition, students might be asked to employ the tools of rhetorical analysis and look primarily at rhetorical context. Like Jezebel, the student who pointed out that the meaning of the "N-word" differs depending on who is saying it and to whom, students might consider how the author and audience influence the contextual meaning of the word or phrase.

In a linguistics class, the instructor might consider asking students to thoroughly trace the etymology and deconstruct the piece of language with regards to phonemics, syntactical and semantic structure, or pragmatics. In a literature course, the instructor might invite students to look at the usage of a particular piece of language in literary works over a given time period or to explore how different authors employ the word or phrase. In a fiction class, students might be directed to frame the essay as a narrative; in a journalism course, the piece may more closely resemble a profile.

BOX 7.3.   WORDS AND PHRASES WITH RACIAL OR RACIST HISTORIES OR BOTH*

Bugger	Hip hip hooray	Redneck
Cakewalk	Hooligan	Shylock
Call a spade a spade	Indian giver	Sold down the river
Eenie meenie miney moe	Long time, no see	Squaw
Eskimo	No can do	The -itis
Ghetto	Paddy wagon	Thug
Grandfather clause/Grandfa-	Peanut gallery	Uppity
thered in	Pickaninny	White trash
Gyp/Gypped/Gypsy	Wigger	
Hooligan		

* Some of these terms originated as racist slurs, while others took on racist usage at a later point in time. The origins of some of these terms remain uncertain.

Like other papers students write, the word biographies should be shared in class either in small peer groups or during short informal share-outs with the whole class. This sharing allows students to learn a little more about the histories of the words their classmates chose. Students can also explain some of their motivation behind selecting a particular word and how their perspective on that word has been influenced by their research. Like Jezebel and Chantel, students may have very different understandings of and feelings about individual words, how they are used, and by whom. Such differences highlight the complexity and fluidity of language and the many factors that influence how an individual employs and perceives language in context.

Discussions of race labels and racialized language can segue—with, perhaps, a little urging on the part of the instructor—into discussions of the situatedness of language, as well as authorial choice and diction in composition. Using these words as reference points, students can consider the ways in which a writer's word selection conveys ideology and perspective. Through writing exercises and peer review, students may then examine their own language use on subjects both sociopolitical and academic. In the racial literacy classroom, the interrogation of terminology around race can be used to initiate discussion of the abilities of language to categorize and identify, as well as to reify, rearrange, and resist.

CONCLUDING THOUGHTS

Racial literacy curricula in the English classroom, now more than ever, need to consider how language itself serves to maintain the existing structures of racial hierarchy in American society and how—through the interrogation of language—we can recognize and challenge that hierarchy. Curricula that heighten racial awareness can have a "ripple effect"[7] by helping to create an environment in which all students, but particularly students of color and other marginalized populations, feel more supported.

Over time, students become more comfortable verbally interrogating the language of not only race and racism but also other significant modes of discrimination and oppression, including sexism, homophobia, and anti-immigrant rhetoric. This is the strongest, too-often-untapped potential of the composition classroom and the clearest reason composition ought to embrace the framework of racial literacy.

NOTES

1. Mica Pollock, *Colormute: Race Talk Dilemmas in an American School* (Princeton: Princeton University Press, 2004), 14.

2. Derald Wing Sue, *Race Talk and the Conspiracy of Silence: Understanding and Facilitating Difficult Dialogues on Race* (Hoboken, NJ: Wiley, 2015), 115.

3. Marc Lamont Hill, *Beats, Rhymes, and Classroom Life: Hip-Hop Pedagogy and the Politics of Identity* (New York: Teachers College Press, 2009), 49.

4. This anecdote is adapted from Mara Lee Grayson, "Race Talk in the College Composition Classroom: Narrative Song Lyrics as Texts for Racial Literacy," *Teaching English in the Two-Year College* 45, no. 2 (2017).

5. Jennifer Clary-Lemon, "The Racialization of Composition Studies: Scholarly Rhetoric of Race since 1990," *College Composition and Communication* 61, no. 2 (2009): 4.

6. Jennifer Beech, "Redneck and Hillbilly Discourse in the Writing Classroom: Classifying Critical Pedagogies of Whiteness," *College English* 67 (2004): 175.

7. Beverly Daniel Tatum, "Talking about Race, Learning about Racism: The Application of Racial Identity Development Theory in the Classroom," *Harvard Educational Review* 62, no. 1 (1992): 23.

8

Racial Literacy as Civic Engagement

Writing beyond the Classroom

> "To affirm that men and women are persons and as persons should be free, and yet to do nothing tangible to make this affirmation a reality, is a farce."
>
> —Paulo Freire[1]

The ideas and skills students learn in college must have applications that reach beyond classroom walls and into their local and global communities. Nowhere is this truer than in the racial literacy classroom. While racial literacy may be considered an analytical framework, it cannot be separated from the lived realities of race and racism and the roles they play in society. Racial literacy educators must therefore encourage students to make connections between the classroom and the world outside of it and use the framework to interrogate injustice, whether inside the academy or past its doors.

RACIAL LITERACY AND ANTIRACISM

Racial literacy educator Yolanda Sealey-Ruiz has lamented that the students in one racial literacy composition classroom she studied "did not move to action—the next preferred step in racial literacy development."[2] In fact, little research into racial literacy in the classroom emphasizes this step as part of the curriculum. Racial literacy research may deemphasize the activist components of the curriculum because of practical curricular concerns. With so much to do *inside* the classroom, teachers may have little time to effectively bring the curriculum *outside* the classroom. Moreover, many instructors do not receive institutional support in the form of funding or departmental encouragement to expand the curriculum to include off-campus excursions or community service activities.

117

Some instructors, especially those who lack the support of their administrations, may forego this component of the curriculum. Some have argued that students' youth may prevent them from being antiracist activists or that one semester simply isn't enough time to move students to action. On the one hand, it is arguable that young people may be less motivated or have fewer resources to take part in antiracist activism. On the other hand, many activist movements are and have historically been youth-based. While a semester is indeed a short period of time given the emotional and analytical depth of the curriculum, instructors can implement in-class activities and, if possible, service-learning opportunities that encourage students to identify and brainstorm methods to rectify inequities in their local communities.

TEACHER RESOURCE: CULTURAL LITERACY DICTIONARIES

Learning about racial inequity may make students begin to question their roles as members of a society in which race and racism play such salient roles. If racial inequity is built into the institutions of life in the United States of America, what does it mean to believe in, say, the American dream? What does it mean to idealize the melting pot once one learns that diversity is not spread out across a level playing field? What does it mean to see equal rights as one of the foremost ideals of American society if one also realizes that all are *not* equal in the fabric of the United States?

Some people believe that, in order to fight against something, one must also fight for something. As such, before students can take action against racism, they may need to identify what it is they want for the worlds they inhabit—and how existing ideologies and institutions uphold those ideals or prevent them from becoming reality. Many of the assignments in the racial literacy classroom invite students to reflect on their own identities and beliefs about the world. It is important that they also reflect on the ideologies of the broader cultures and communities of which they are a part.

To take an antiracist activist stance outside of the classroom, students must begin to turn their critical gaze outward. In the racial literacy classroom, students can build their own "cultural literacy" dictionaries based on E. D. Hirsch's controversial text *Cultural Literacy*[3] to start to identify what is valued in the United States, as well as what should be valued but isn't.

A Brief Background on Cultural Literacy

All texts presume some prior knowledge on the part of readers. To understand the references in and contexts surrounding a piece of literature, one may need to know historical information, like notable names and events, or have some familiarity with other literary texts. References to popular culture or current events may lose their relevance over time. For example, a story written in 1969 or 1970 that references the Days of Rage might have enabled readers of that time (and of a particular political orientation) to connect with the text. In 2017, however, readers unfamiliar with the series of Chicago demonstrations against the Vietnam War might gloss over the reference and miss important contextual elements of the story or feel alienated from the text.

In the mid-1980s, when much educational research explored the necessity of critical thinking and culturally inclusive pedagogies geared toward improving the educational experiences of students from racially, linguistically, and socioeconomically nondominant backgrounds, University of Virginia professor of education and humanities E. D. Hirsch published the seminal text *Cultural Literacy*, which explored the idea that there were pieces of background information necessary for American readers to know in order to approach a text that assumes from readers a certain foundational knowledge. This background included historical names, dates, and places; textual references; cultural symbols; and such linguistic elements as idioms.

Hirsch claimed that cultural knowledge was foundational in nonacademic life as well and acknowledged that Americans must already possess a considerable body of cultural knowledge simply to get through the day. For example, one must know on which side of the street to drive and how to get to his or her desired location. Hirsch argued that critical thinking alone was not sufficient to ensure students' success inside or outside of the classroom and criticized the lack of background information regularly taught to the student population. While critical thinking may be a valuable focus in the field of education, no amount of it could teach students the facts and foundational knowledge that afford them the ability to *apply* that critical thinking to their educational experiences or daily lives.

Returning to the example of the driver: If he attempts to drive straight but encounters a roadblock, he does not simply turn his car around and return home; instead, he considers an alternative route. Perhaps, for example, he makes a right turn to avoid the obstacle up ahead. While this ordinary example highlights the commonness of critical thinking in daily life, the driver's problem cannot be solved without cultural knowledge as well as critical thinking. If that driver is unaware, for example, that in New York City one cannot turn right on a red light, then he risks being ticketed as he attempts to problem-solve and alter his course.

More broadly, Hirsch argued that cultural knowledge was a prerequisite for academic success and social progress and suggested that even those who sought to subvert the status quo of American life employed more conservative rhetoric in order to make their ideas more palatable to a mainstream audience. He pointed to the newspaper *The Black Panther* as an example of a text that was "radical in sentiment but more conservative in its language and cultural assumptions."[4] Excerpts he identified included references to particular phrases, facts, and ideologies that indicated a "rigorous traditional education"[5] in the fields of American history, grammar, and Bible studies, just to name a few. At the end of the book Hirsch included a list of people, places, and terms he believed all Americans should know in order to achieve cultural literacy.

If the list was problematic (see box 8.1), then the intention was equitable. Cultural illiteracy may in fact compound the academic problems faced by those who,

BOX 8.1.   SO WHAT WAS THE PROBLEM?

Despite what many have seen as Hirsch's equitable intentions, the list of names, words, and concepts he included as necessary for Americans to know was heavy on the "'dead white males' who had formed the foundations of American culture but who had by then begun to fall out of academic fashion."[a] For example, while the term *Black Muslims* is identified as one of the phrases every American should know—and despite the fact that Hirsch uses *The Black Panther* newspaper as a key example in his book—the term *Black Panther* is noticeably absent from Hirsch's list, as are names like Huey Newton and Bobby Seale, an inconsistency that seems to devalue influential people of color.

As such, Hirsch's work evoked a cultural ideology that failed to address either the diverse American population or contemporary educational scholarship. While Hirsch believed that this enterprise would provide poor and underserved populations the cultural capital needed to succeed in the academy and beyond, his theory and dictionary were largely interpreted as advocating a return to the White cultural hegemonic traditions of the academy rather than opening the academy to diverse perspectives and experiences.

---

a. Eric Liu, "What Every American Should Know: Defining Common Cultural Literacy for an Increasingly Diverse Nation," *The Atlantic*, July 3, 2015.

by virtue of their skin color, home language, or socioeconomic status, have been underserved by their earlier educational experiences. Therefore, by improving their cultural literacy, people from nondominant groups in American society are better able to communicate in the language of power with the vocabulary of the dominant.

Improving one's cultural literacy cannot, of course, correct for the inequities of our systems of education and governance, particularly where race is concerned, but "any endeavor that makes it easier for those who do not know the memes and themes of American civic life to attain them closes the opportunity gap."[6] This is especially important in a changing United States, where non-Whites may soon be the majority yet where power structures will likely continue to remain White-dominated.

The Classroom Cultural Literacy Dictionary

To fulfill the unrealized potential of Hirsch's cultural literacy, his work could serve as the foundation for a new cultural literacy dictionary, one in which the experiences and perspectives of diverse groups of non-White Americans are celebrated. In the racial literacy classroom, crafting the cultural literacy dictionary requires students to explore how language represents, reifies, and resists cultural ideology.

Building the Dictionary

Before attempting to draft their own dictionaries, students must read excerpts from Hirsch's book and some of the scholarly responses to the book, including reviews (positive and negative) and works that build on the framework he developed. These readings provide the background needed to envision this assignment not only as an entertaining activity but also as an academic endeavor with a complex history. After students read these excerpts (and perhaps write a commentary or two to more fully explore the ideas), they should create their own lists of important terms or concepts people in the United States should know today. To keep the assignment manageable and to encourage students to prioritize, each dictionary should include no more than ten entries. In addition to listing the terms, students should include a brief definition of each term, as well as a short (one paragraph) justification for its inclusion in the dictionary (see box 8.2).

BOX 8.2. QUESTIONS TO HELP STUDENTS BUILD THEIR DICTIONARIES

1. What do you think it means to be an American?
2. What do you wish other people in this country knew about your culture, race, and ethnicity?
3. What customs or traditions are celebrated in this country?
4. What customs or traditions do you think should be celebrated?
5. What do you remember learning about the history of the United States of America?
6. What do you wish you learned as a child about U.S. history?
7. If a tourist asked you for recommendations, what would you suggest as must-sees in the United States?
8. What do you like about living in the United States?
9. What don't you like about living in the United States?
10. What problems or struggles seem unique to the United States?
11. Have you ever traveled outside the United States? What did you miss most?
12. If you were born or have lived outside the United States, what is the biggest difference you noticed between here and there?

To highlight the inclusive nature of the assignment, these dictionaries should be shared. Therefore, instead of turning them in to the teacher, students should read and discuss their entries in small in-class groups or, better yet, post their entries to a shared online discussion board (such as Blackboard, Moodle, or another distance-learning platform). Students can discuss and even debate in class or in writing the terms and concepts they believe to be most significant to an American identity. Students can then, as a class, work to build one larger, more comprehensive cultural literacy dictionary, incorporating the suggestions and rationale of all members of the class.

What to Expect

> In his racial literacy classroom, Cesar, an international student from Mexico, chose as one of his cultural literacy dictionary entries the word *culture*, which his teacher had previously defined in class as the complex and dynamic shared patterns of behavior and language of a group of people who interact over time.[7] Cesar wrote that it was important for American culture to assimilate the "different points of view from people of other cultures." Another entry in Cesar's dictionary was *American*: "The United States is only part of North America," he wrote.

Some students will immediately take a critical approach to the assignment. In the example shared here, Cesar's entry is so interesting, not because of the word *culture* itself, but because of his explanation of the term. He uses the word *assimilate*, which is generally used to describe the acts of those who attempt to fit into American society, to describe the actions the broader society must take to integrate diverse peoples into the culture of the United States. By flipping the use of the word, so to speak, Cesar uses politicized language to express a political statement.

This statement demonstrates not only Cesar's understanding of White cultural hegemony but also that this awareness has in fact contributed to the diction he employs in his writing. By also using the dictionary to clarify that the term *American*, as prevalent as it may be in writings inside and outside the academy, is an inaccurate label for a national identification, Cesar further demonstrates his awareness of the ways language reifies cultural ideology. Students like Cesar may use the cultural literacy dictionary to redefine existing terminology or to identify the limitations of preexisting cultural ideologies.

It is very likely, however, that many students' dictionaries will feature predictable symbols of American culture, such as the Declaration of Independence, Thanksgiving, the bald eagle, and the national anthem—after all, these are some of the most visible representations of Americana. Other students may use the cultural literacy dictionary to reiterate the ideals they have been taught to believe that the United States is built on: freedom of speech, the pursuit of happiness, justice for all. Some of these terms may express students' beliefs in American ideology—an ideology that sustains rather than challenges systemic racism.

Racial literacy educators may initially feel frustrated by such responses, but these are wonderful jumping-off points for discussion: Has the United States fulfilled its promise to ensure justice for all Americans? When has freedom of speech been compromised? How is the Thanksgiving story taught to children? How is it taught in college? From a postcolonial perspective? Each entry provides an opportunity for the sort of critical discussion that defines the racial literacy curriculum.

Why It Works

To examine and identify what it means to be American, students must grapple with cultural ideology and personal belief; by reading and discussing their peers' lists as well as their own, they consider where their own beliefs parallel larger American ideologies, as well as the points of disjunction. The activity encourages students to explore the complexity of national and cultural identity. Moreover, by drawing their gaze outward, they are able to identify the more systemic elements of racism, bringing the curriculum beyond the personal and into the structural depths where inequity is created and perpetuated.

Like many other activities in the racial literacy curriculum, the cultural literacy dictionary also helps teachers to see how their students make sense of the material and to adjust the curriculum to meet students' needs. For example, one of the foremost tenets of racial literacy is the recognition that racism is also a contemporary rather than a solely historical problem. If students resist the notion of racism as a pressing, current issue deserving of critical inquiry and concern, then teachers will have to employ a set of texts that establish that foundation. Their entries may alternatively demonstrate the need for additional curricular emphasis on other core concepts of racial literacy, like structural inequity, White privilege, and individual identity and positionality.

INSTRUCTIONAL STRATEGY:
THE PROBLEM-SOLVING GROUP PROJECT

Every semester, Rachel, an English professor at a suburban community college, assigned her composition students a reading autobiography, in which she asked them to reflect on their earliest experiences of reading, being read to, or learning about books. The assignment, she believed, invited students to consider the social and cultural influences behind and implications of reading and other literacy practices. One semester, the students in Rachel's class began to wonder if nurturing literacy could have beneficial social consequences. Working with her students and another colleague, Rachel organized a campus initiative that resulted in the donation of five hundred books to two community institutions: a county jail and a juvenile detention center.

While teaching a Writing in the Disciplines class in a racially diverse private university, Brice assigned his students, mostly juniors and seniors already enrolled in major-level courses, to interview someone employed in their fields of interest. The students had been reading a variety of profile pieces from popular magazines and trade newspapers, and after they conducted their interviews, their next assign-

ment was to write a profile piece on the person they interviewed. At the end of
the semester, Brice compiled the profiles into one manuscript and, using limited
funding provided by his department, published a book. He distributed copies
free of charge to all the students in his class and to other faculty members in his
department.

The frustration and feelings of powerlessness that accompany learning about injustice
may leave many students wondering what they can do to effect change. While some
institutions offer service-learning opportunities, many racial literacy educators will
not have the resources or support to integrate that component into their curricula.
As such, instructors may want to create assignments that inspire students to channel
that frustration. Introducing projects that encourage students to consider actions
they might take outside the classroom may make students feel as though they have
agency—whether they ultimately take the actions identified or not—and they may
even be more motivated to initiate or continue that work once the semester ends.

Working in groups, students can draft a proposal (to be written or multimodally
shared) suggesting a potential way to address an instance of injustice or inequity
they have witnessed on campus or in their communities. Problems on university
campuses that have inspired student activism include microaggressions, culturally
insensitive Halloween party costumes, and defunding of school clubs or organizations. Working in groups encourages collaboration as well as the consideration and
incorporation of multiple perspectives on any given problem. This is an integral
part of the assignment, as it can model for students the difficulty of identifying and
implementing a solution that satisfies all members of a society (or, in this case, a
work group).

The form of the proposal should be tailored to the needs of the course and its
students. In a technical or professional writing course, the written product may
resemble a recommendation report or business proposal. In a class with a large
population of performing arts students or a playwriting course, students might use
more embodied approaches, such as improvisation, scene study, or spoken word,
as a means through which to address and provide constructive suggestions, if not
solutions, for difficult interpersonal and structural problems they face. In a political
science course, students might write letters to their local elected officials.

In higher-level research-based courses, especially in colleges and universities where
undergraduate research and faculty–student collaboration are encouraged, students
can draft proposals for inquiry-based projects to potentially submit to the university's grants office or institutional review board. Students may even be encouraged to
submit their proposals to administrators or, if time and funding allow, present their
proposals at a departmental or university-wide workshop.

In the two examples at the start of this section, educators teaching different classes
in different settings found unique ways to bring their curricula outside the classroom.
While neither Rachel nor Brice were explicitly teaching a racial literacy curriculum,
both instructors' pedagogical choices operate tacitly within the framework and have

important implications for the racial literacy classroom. Rachel's case was successful because not only was she able to secure the institutional support needed to provide the books to the prison, but she also was able to connect the civic-engagement activity back to the classroom curriculum. Students' learning inspired them to take action in their community, and following those activities, students reflected on the ways their engagement with the prison library project influenced their understanding of reading and other literacy practices.

In Brice's class, interviewing individuals in different lines of work not only helped students learn more about their intended fields of work or study, but it also helped to humanize each profession by giving voice to the experiences of members of those disciplines. Moreover, because students used their own language to share those individuals' stories, they had to consider questions of representation. Finally, students were able to see the fruits of their labor in print; the efforts they had made resulted in something tangible. That the tangible evidence was a book, a form that, in academia, has traditionally omitted the voices and perspectives of students of color, makes the project even more significant.

In a more explicit racial literacy curriculum, students might ask their interviewees to reflect on how race, power, and identity play out in their fields and affect their careers. In the sharing of those stories, therefore, each student's positionality becomes even more significant. How does one interpret another's story? How does one retell that story? What is important? What is not? This activity is best used toward the end of the semester, once students have a clear grasp of the concept of positionality and are better prepared to consider how their own experiences and beliefs influence their approach to their interview subjects.

AT SEMESTER'S END

By the end of a racial literacy semester, some students may find that the racial literacy curriculum has helped them to identify available means of antiracist activism and perhaps even undertake steps to turn their ideas into action. Others may reach the end of the semester unready or unwilling to take those steps. Instructors must remember that racial literacy is a journey rather than an end point. All students, from the hesitant racial literacy students to those poised to fight injustice (and any in between), must be reminded of this, as well. On the last day of class, instructors might even consider providing all students with a list of potential next steps they can take or further resources they may review after they leave the classroom. (The resources listed at the end of this book might be helpful to include on this list.)

Students who have struggled with the curriculum may leave the course unsure of what they really learned or why it mattered. Rather than be discouraged by this stagnancy, instructors should encourage students to keep open minds as they reflect on the work they did over the course of the semester. Last-day activities may include small- or large-group discussions reflecting on what students learned, what still confuses or troubles them, what they felt throughout the semester, and how they feel finishing the semester; planning sessions to help students consider how they might be able to incorporate the concepts of racial literacy into their classwork and their academic careers moving forward; and informal course evaluations (best done anonymously), which instructors can review as they plan their curricula for the next academic term.

Students who conclude the term with plans for action may feel especially determined, euphoric, or enlightened—but these heightened emotions do not paint a complete picture of the work racial literacy continues to require. Despite their newfound critical consciousness, students must continue to reflect, critique, and analyze (and repeat), inside and outside of the academy. With care not to dash these students' hopes or positivity, instructors should remind students of the struggles they will continue to face as they move through their schooling, careers, and personal lives as racialized individuals in an inequitable society.

CONCLUDING THOUGHTS

Students must define for themselves what activism means to them and how they might become agents for change in their own communities. Such a definition, however, is complex and subject to change as an individual has new experiences and gains new knowledge. The definition changes because it must change as people, conditions, and societies shift. Even a working definition can take a lifetime to articulate.

Teachers, too, must remain open to inspiration and change as they consider how they serve as antiracist activists. While some educators sign petitions, organize rallies, or take to the streets during public demonstrations or protests, others find their activist voices inside the academy. On individual campuses, instructors may serve on faculty committees geared toward equitable admissions or hiring practices, they can volunteer to work with on-campus social justice initiatives, or they may offer to mentor student groups with similar missions. Off campus, most professional teaching organizations have special-interest groups and caucuses that work to create more inclusive, culturally responsive curricula and pedagogy; increase opportunities for students and educators of color; and further social justice initiatives in educational institutions and in the profession itself.

Racial literacy educators, so many of whom are blessed and cursed with the insatiable desire to effect change and improve the education and lives of the students in their care, are likely to feel like they can never do enough. At times like these, it is important to pause for a moment to consider the work one is doing and how many students are influenced by that work, whether those students realize it at the time or not. Some students may not recognize the import of what they have experienced in the racial literacy classroom until long after they have left it. It can be hard on instructors to watch students leave at the end of any semester, but those feelings

BOX 8.3.   SUPPORTING STUDENTS (AND YOURSELF) AFTER THE SEMESTER ENDS

- **Be available.** Students may want to e-mail you or visit your office to reflect on the course or share something they have newly discovered about themselves. Because of the intimacy of the curriculum, students may trust you more than other faculty members. While you will, of course, have new students to deal with, it's a good idea to allow a little time for students who still need to process after the semester ends. That said, remember that you can, if necessary, refer them elsewhere.
- **Reflect and regroup.** You'll give a lot during the semester. After it ends, self-care is of utmost importance. Confide in a trusted colleague, friend, or family member about the struggles you faced during the semester. Relive the successes of the curriculum, the progress your students made, and the joy and pride you felt watching your students grow. Make sure you are eating well, sleeping well, and doing things you enjoy outside the classroom.
- **Begin again.** Once you've dedicated yourself to this curriculum, you'll likely be teaching it again. Consider what worked; what didn't; and what you'd like to add, take away, or change. Instead of relying on the same syllabus each semester, take some time to make the changes that make you more confident in the curriculum. You'll enter the new semester more prepared to handle familiar challenges—and tackle new ones.

can be compounded by the emotional intensity and intimacy of the racial literacy curriculum.

Teaching is always a political act. What one decides to teach, the pedagogies one employs, one's theories of learning, even how one arranges chairs in a classroom—all of these are political decisions influenced by an educator's beliefs about a society, its people, its body of knowledge, and how that knowledge is disseminated among those people. When thoughtful, student-responsive, and equitable, teaching can also be an act of resistance. At a time when so many voices are silenced, either directly or through structural inequities that make it impossible for those voices to be heard, teachers, more than ever, must see themselves as teacher-activists.

NOTES

1. Paulo Freire, *Pedagogy of the Oppressed*, 30th anniversary ed. (New York: Bloomsbury Academic, 2000).

2. Yolanda Sealey-Ruiz, "Building Racial Literacy in First-Year Composition," *Teaching English in the Two-Year College* 40, no. 4 (2013): 394.

3. E. D. Hirsch Jr., *Cultural Literacy: What Every American Should Know* (New York: Vintage, 1987).

4. Ibid., 22.

5. Ibid., 23.

6. Eric Liu, "What Every American Should Know: Defining Common Cultural Literacy for an Increasingly Diverse Nation," *The Atlantic*, July 3, 2015.

7. See John W. Creswell, *Qualitative Inquiry and Research Design: Choosing among Five Approaches*, 3rd ed. (Los Angeles: Sage, 2013); and Brian Street, "Culture Is a Verb," in *Language and Culture: Papers from the Annual Meeting of the British Association of Applied Linguistics, Held at Trevelyan College, University of Durham, September 1991*, eds. David Graddol, Linda Thompson, and Mike Byram (Clevedon, UK: British Association for Applied Linguistics in association with Multilingual Matters, 1993).

9

Special Considerations for Secondary English Education

"If only we got that kind of exposure in high school."

—Kelly, university freshman

One of the reasons many college students embrace the opportunity to openly discuss race, racism, and racialism is because such an opportunity has not arisen earlier in their academic careers. This is an especially troubling component of the racial literacy curriculum and one that teachers ought to be cognizant of as they craft their curricula. The first year of college should not be anyone's academic introduction to the issues of race, racism, racialization, and antiracism, all of which have long affected students' lives, either without their awareness or with their awareness but without direct discussion. It is imperative that we offer racial literacy curricula while our students are still in high school.

Because many students are raised in homogeneous environments in which they have "few substantive interactions with diverse peers . . . the undergraduate environment provides critical and unique opportunities to engage in novel interactions with racially/ethnically diverse peers and form meaningful interpersonal relationships."[1] Given that public schooling in the United States remains practically, if not legally, racially segregated, college students who attend schools outside their communities may find themselves interacting for the first time with classmates whose backgrounds differ from their own.

However, because two-year and community colleges generally reflect, both in population and curriculum, the needs and culture of the surrounding communities, students in these schools may never encounter such racial and ethnic diversity. This confirms the necessity of bringing racial literacy education to students before they leave high school.

Much educational research of the late twentieth and early twenty-first centuries has emphasized equitable, culturally relevant approaches to literacy curricula for students in predominantly Black public schools. However, assuming racial literacy to be suited solely—or even primarily—for Black students is reductive and ignores the enormous potential of the racial literacy curriculum for students of all racial and ethnic identities. Moreover, while students of all races and ethnicities have been shown to benefit from diversity and interracial interaction, White students have been shown to benefit more from this introduction to diversity than students of color.[2] As such, it may be especially important for students in predominantly White high schools to experience racial literacy curricula prior to attending college.

While the particulars may differ, teaching and learning are far more human and interpersonal than they are generational. The lines that divide a twelfth-grade high-schooler from a college freshman, for example, are far blurrier than the institutions would lead us to believe. Many high schools offer Advanced Placement credits or college-learning options for high-achieving students, and many community colleges offer GED preparatory classes for students who have not earned high school diplomas. The path to—and through—higher education is not necessarily a linear one. As such, there is no reason similar approaches would not be just as successful in the high school classroom.

That said, teaching racial literacy in the high school setting comes with unique concerns and requires instructors attend to additional considerations. Teachers considering implementing racial literacy curricula should be prepared to face these challenges—and others—when they enter the classroom.

POTENTIAL OBSTACLES

The demands of standardized testing, along with other institutional and ideological constraints of secondary education, may prevent instructors from teaching (and students from experiencing) English language arts (ELA) curricula that tackle issues of racism and racialism head on. The likeliest sources of tension in the secondary school are curriculum, administration, and students' parents. These obstacles are connected, of course, and trouble in one area is likely to increase trouble in another. By the same token, once one problem has been addressed, the others are likely to fall in line.

Curricular Concerns

Given limited time during the schoolyear to cope with the pressures of Common Core State Standards (CCSS), end-of-year testing, and teacher evaluation systems based more on students' test scores than teachers' qualifications, instructors may wonder how they can possibly bring in a racial literacy curriculum without taking away from other, seemingly more pressing issues. On the one hand, race and racism can seem like the most pressing matters in the world to racial literacy educators; on the other, compared to the consequences of students failing state exams or teachers being fired, the racial literacy curriculum can seem rather abstract and out of touch with the realities of the classroom (which is, of course, the opposite of its true aims).

Administrative Anxiety

Educational administrators in public and private high schools manage budgets; liaise with parents, teachers, community members, board members, and legislators; and ensure that curricular objectives adhere to the guidelines set forth by public or private accreditation bodies. Most administrators, however, lack the content knowledge that enable faculty members to develop sound curricula and pedagogies.

Sometimes concerns unrelated to curriculum unduly influence the curricula sanctioned by the school administration. Time constraints and lack of funding for professional development may deter school administrations from approving racial literacy curricula. Faced with what they see as a sensitive and potentially controversial curriculum, they may reason that adequate training is required to ensure that teachers do no harm to students and make as few waves as possible with parents. They may want to set guidelines for the implementation of the curriculum to prevent teachers from straying too far into political or otherwise incendiary territory. Problematically, because administrators are not typically classroom teachers, even if they do take the time to develop these guidelines, the guidelines themselves may not match the needs of the classroom or its students.

Parental Interference

Some teachers who bring discussions of race into high school classrooms have found themselves dealing with complaints from parents uncomfortable with the "political" nature of this instruction. Some parents, especially those who themselves were raised to avoid race talk, may feel that it is improper for their children to discuss race in the classroom, particularly when they are not present. Others will not understand why the curriculum is significant or relevant. Those who have not addressed questions of racial inequity or White privilege may not understand the exigency of such curricula. Finally, there are those parents who will object to the curriculum because they don't believe race and racism matter. These parents may see the curriculum as inappropriate or politicized and may even accuse the teacher of "having an agenda."

NECESSARY PRECAUTIONS

While these challenges may seem daunting, they should not deter thoughtful, equity-minded educators from teaching a racial literacy curriculum on the high school level. The following are a few precautions that may be taken to keep the curriculum running as smoothly as possible.

Make Curricular Connections

In order to work racial literacy into the curriculum and provide for the immediate and long-term needs of the students in the classroom, teachers must find tangible ways to weave the framework into their instruction. The ninth-grader who needs to pass a reading-comprehension and essay-writing exam at the end of the year may be better served by discussing a short reading about racism with his classmates than learning explicitly about racial literacy's origins in civil rights law and sociology.

Additionally, despite the controversy that has surrounded the CCSS since its implementation, it is conceivable for teachers to do the work of teaching racial literacy using the guidelines the standards provide. For example, New York State CCSS for ELA emphasizes improving students' abilities to analyze and interpret various types of texts, including digital media and visual content; identifying and evaluating the central claims of any text; and understanding the differences between what a text says directly and what a text implies.[3] These skills are also foundational to the racial literacy curriculum.

While the CCSS includes some content requirements for ELA, such as significant texts in American literature and classical mythology, the requirements of the CCSS apply more to skill sets than course content. It is, therefore, possible to adhere to CCSS while using texts and pedagogies more relevant to the racial literacy curriculum. Teachers, especially when working with older students, can even ask students how they feel about the texts read. Did they feel represented in the texts provided? Which texts do they wish they could read in the classroom? Such questions require reflection on matters of identity, textual representation, and representation in education, thereby practicing (directly or obliquely) the critical skills of racial literacy.

Involve the Parents

Parental interference is not always a result of racism or ire; in many cases, parents simply don't know enough about the curriculum or the framework of racial literacy to know what to expect. Therefore, the best way to get parents onboard is to keep them informed about the curriculum and involve them in class activities however possible.

At the beginning of—or even before—the school year, instructors should send welcome letters to parents, introducing themselves and the racial literacy curriculum. The welcome letter might include background on the framework of racial literacy, information on the connections between racial literacy and the course material students are studying, a preview of some activities students will complete during the school year, and perhaps even a few links to racial literacy classroom research. Teachers might also want to include a contact number where parents can reach them with any questions.

It is important, however, to differentiate between a welcome letter and what is essentially a permission slip. If teachers ask parents for consent to teach this curriculum, then there is always a chance some parents will *not* consent—and there is no way to teach this curriculum to half a class. Moreover, asking for permission implies that there is a danger to the curriculum. While the letter must provide context and a rationale for the curriculum in order to help parents understand its necessity, this welcome letter should set out to normalize racial literacy education as much as possible.

While students may bristle at the idea of their parents being involved in their schoolwork, it is a good idea to keep parents involved throughout the school year. Through students' assignments, including the racial autobiography and positionality cluster maps, teachers can invite parents to contribute to curricula. As students explore their individual racial and ethnic identities, they can gain valuable insights by asking their parents about their ethnic heritage, their experiences with race and racism, and other elements of a family history. For racial literacy to be meaningful inside and outside the classroom, connections must be made between home life and school life. As such, by involving the parents, teachers can both ensure parental co-operation and make racial literacy a richer experience for students.

Involve the School

It is a familiar pattern: Unhappy parent complains to administration; administrator reproaches teacher; teacher modifies (or dismantles) part of curriculum for fear of retaliation. If the school is involved (meaning departmental personnel and school administration are informed and, ideally, supportive of instruction), then there is a better chance that a teacher will be protected if parents consider his or her curriculum to be controversial. In order to get school administrators onboard, racial literacy educators should consider how projects conducted in the classroom can benefit the larger school community.

Teachers might consider, for example, concluding the academic year with an extracurricular activity inspired by the curriculum, such as a play or variety show to be attended by students, faculty, and parents. Students can present the findings of their research or problem-solving projects through performances like poetry slams, short plays, improvised scene work, or musical performances.

Alternatively, teachers can help students organize after-school workshops that encourage students from all over the school to participate in components of the racial literacy curriculum that are relevant to their experiences on campus. Embodied approaches to microaggressions and interracial dating, for example, may help students to metaphorically step into another's shoes and make tangible ideas and concerns that might seem abstract, thereby improving interpersonal relations within the school community. It may also be necessary to identify ways racial literacy curricula might reach beyond school walls and into local communities.

Make Connections with the Community

To establish relevance for students, parents, and administrators, connections between the racial literacy curriculum and the surrounding community should be clearly established. Creating programs that use the skills students develop in the classroom to reach out into local neighborhoods makes explicit the ways classroom instruction prepares students for future academic success as well as civic engagement. Possible community projects include participant action research projects to help students address problems they see in their own communities; fund-raising for underfunded community organizations; service-learning initiatives that invite students to volunteer at local shelters, hospitals, or community centers; and performances to be attended by local residents, as well as parents and faculty. (More information on racial literacy activities that bridge the classroom and community can be found in chapter 8.)

CONCLUDING THOUGHTS

No racial literacy curriculum, whether in a college composition classroom or on a public high school campus, will be an effortless endeavor. To assume it will be is a misunderstanding of the nature of racial literacy and an underestimation of the deeply seated structural and emotionalized individual components of race and racism in contemporary society. However, the more support racial literacy educators, be they high school teachers or college professors, have in their corners, the more positive the journey will be. Fewer distractions and administrative obstacles mean more time can be spent developing the curriculum and implementing practices to help students practice racial literacy and improve their analytical and critical writing skills. With administrative and parental support, instructors' focus can remain on the classroom, where it belongs.

NOTES

1. Nicholas A. Bowman and Nida Denson, "What's Past Is Prologue: How Precollege Exposure to Racial Diversity Shapes the Impact of College Interracial Interactions," *Research in Higher Education* 53 (2012): 407.

2. Ibid.

3. *New York State P–12 Common Core Learning Standards for English Language Arts and Literacy*, January 10, 2011, http://schools.nyc.gov/NR/rdonlyres/337BF93A-95FF-4A48 -9434-CE9EA0B70E06/0/p12common_core_learning_standards_ela_final.pdf.

Afterword

Teaching racial literacy is, for lack of a better word, a calling, and it should not be entered into lightly. In the years I have been doing this work, I have experienced struggles and setbacks, as well as successes that make any of those obstacles worth the effort. If you have picked up this book, I believe that you, too, are drawn to this work and are willing to take the steps needed to enter into this endeavor with me.

My aim in writing this book is not to prescribe a single best practice for the teaching of racial literacy but instead to offer the fullest picture I can—based on the anecdotal and empirical data I have collected over the years—of the most useful pedagogical tools available to would-be racial literacy educators. The only constant of racial literacy instruction, like all good teaching, is change. We must be willing to adapt to best meet the needs of our students and the new knowledge and discoveries of our disciplines. Social, cultural, and political changes also demand that racial literacy educators find new ways to address the inequities that have too often defined life in the United States of America.

Writing this, I cannot ignore the fact that the current president of the United States has spent his brief time in office introducing racist legislation and supporting, both verbally and through law, racist rhetoric and violence. It is important to remember, however, that while Donald Trump lost the popular vote, he was elected through the established means that govern the elections of those who govern us. Those means, which include but are not limited to the electoral college, voter ID laws, and gerrymandering (with some contribution from immigration law and the workings of the prison industrial complex), have long contributed to the disenfranchisement of voters of color, immigrants, impoverished citizens, and other minoritized populations.

While many people have expressed shock at the emergence of hate speech and racist violence that have accompanied Trump's presidency, many of us who do this work were not surprised. Racism is not new, and while it had perhaps been pushed beneath the surface of public discourse, it has not reemerged now so much as it has simply made itself more visible to the general public. The truth is more troubling to admit: Racism is in fact a defining characteristic of the institutions that uphold our way of life in the United States.

Equally troubling is that, despite Trump's inequitable legislation and the fact that he is currently under investigation for financial connections with Russia during his presidential campaign, many Americans, particularly working-class White people, continue to support Trump and his cabinet. More than fifty years ago, Bob Dylan told the story of the assassination of Black civil rights leader Medgar Evers to describe how politicians have used racism to silence the voices of poor White Americans (see the second verse of Dylan's song "Only a Pawn in Their Game"). Critical race theory calls this *interest convergence*: White elites benefit materially from racism, whereas poor Whites benefit psychically.[1] That so many of those who are disadvantaged by the racialized workings of American society turn a blind eye to racism cements the necessity of bringing racial literacy curricula to even those sites that are seemingly least likely to embrace it.

This new political era demands an even more rigorous approach to addressing race, racism, and social (in)justice. Students in our classrooms must learn more than the prescribed sets of skills sanctioned by testing companies and sought by corporations. Students must learn what a formal education affords them—and what it doesn't. They must learn what it means to be citizens, not in the legal sense of the word, but in the civic one, as members of a society that is at once diverse and inequitable. They must learn more about their classmates, and they must learn more about themselves. Racial literacy will not, on its own, solve the inequities of our society or its educational institutions. But it may help us, and our students, name them.

NOTE

1. Richard Delgado and Jean Stefancic, *Critical Race Theory: An Introduction*, 2nd ed. (New York: New York University Press, 2012), 8.

References and Additional Resources for Instructors and Students

RESOURCES FOR EDUCATORS

The texts listed in this section provide additional information about the racial literacy framework, its theoretical influences, and its potential for educational practice and pedagogy.

The Racial Literacy Framework

Guinier, Lani. "Admissions Rituals as Political Acts: Guardians at the Gate of Our Democratic Ideals." *Harvard Law Review* (2003).

Guinier, Lani. "From Racial Liberalism to Racial Literacy: *Brown v. Board of Education* and the Interest-Divergence Dilemma." *Journal of American History* 91, no. 1 (2004): 92–118.

Twine, France Winddance. *A White Side of Black Britain: Interracial Intimacy and Racial Literacy.* Durham, NC: Duke University Press, 2010.

Twine, France Winddance. "A White Side of Black Britain: The Concept of Racial Literacy." *Ethnic and Racial Studies* 27, no. 6 (2004): 878–907.

Race and Structural Racism

Coates, Ta-Nehisi. "There Is No Post-Racial America." *The Atlantic* (July/August 2015).

Delgado, Richard, and Jean Stefancic. *Critical Race Theory: An Introduction.* 2nd ed. New York: New York University Press, 2012.

Morning, Ann. "Ethnic Classification in Global Perspective: A Cross-National Survey of the 2000 Census Round." *United Nations.org.* Last modified August 10, 2005. https://unstats.un.org/unsd/demographic/sconcerns/popchar/Morning.pdf.

Omi, Michael, and Howard Winant. *Racial Formation in the United States: From the 1960s to the 1990s.* 2nd ed. New York: Routledge, 1994.

Sue, Derald Wing. *Race Talk and the Conspiracy of Silence: Understanding and Facilitating Difficult Dialogues on Race.* Hoboken, NJ: Wiley, 2015.

United States Census Bureau. "Race—About." *Census.gov*. Last modified July 8, 2013. http://www.census.gov/topics/population/race/about.html.

Wellman, David T. *Portraits of White Racism*. 2nd ed. Cambridge: Cambridge University Press, 1993.

Wise, Tim. *Colorblind: The Rise of Post-Racial Politics and the Retreat from Racial Equity*. San Francisco: City Lights, 2010.

Race and Education

Bowman, Nicholas A., and Nida Denson. "What's Past Is Prologue: How Precollege Exposure to Racial Diversity Shapes the Impact of College Interracial Interactions." *Research in Higher Education* 53 (2012): 406–25.

Clary-Lemon, Jennifer. "The Racialization of Composition Studies: Scholarly Rhetoric of Race since 1990." *College Composition and Communication* 61, no. 2 (2009): 1–17.

Conference on College Composition and Communication. "Students' Right to Their Own Language." *College Composition and Communication* 25 (1974).

Johnston-Guerrero, Marc P. "The Meanings of Race Matter: College Students Learning about Race in a Not-So-Postracial Era." *American Educational Research Journal* 53, no. 4 (2016).

Kirkland, David E. "'The Rose That Grew from Concrete': Postmodern Blackness and New English Education." *English Journal* 97, no. 5 (2008): 69–75.

Ladson-Billings, Gloria. "But That's Just Good Teaching! The Case for Culturally Relevant Pedagogy." *Theory into Practice* 34, no. 3 (1995): 159–65.

Nieto, Sonia M. "Profoundly Multicultural Questions." *Equity and Opportunity* 60, no. 4 (2003): 6–10.

Pollock, Mica. *Colormute: Race Talk Dilemmas in an American School*. Princeton: Princeton University Press, 2004.

Prendergast, Catherine. "Race: The Absent Presence in Composition Studies." *College Composition and Communication* 50, no. 1 (1998): 36–53.

Singleton, Glenn E., and Curtis Linton. *Courageous Conversations about Race: A Field Guide for Achieving Equity in Schools*. Thousand Oaks, CA: Corwin, 2006.

Smitherman, Geneva. "'Students' Right to Their Own Language': A Retrospective." *English Journal* 84, no. 1 (1995): 21–27.

Racial Literacy in Teacher Education

Rogers, Rebecca, and Melissa Mosley. "A Critical Discourse Analysis of Racial Literacy in Teacher Education." *Linguistics and Education: An International Research Journal* 19, no. 2 (2008): 107–31.

Sealey-Ruiz, Yolanda. "Dismantling the School-to-Prison Pipeline through Racial Literacy Development in Teacher Education." *Journal of Curriculum and Pedagogy* 8, no. 2 (2011): 116–20.

Sealey-Ruiz, Yolanda, and Perry Greene. "Popular Visual Images and the (Mis)Reading of Black Male Youth: A Case for Racial Literacy in Urban Preservice Teacher Education." *Teaching Education* 26, no. 1 (2015): 55–76.

Skerrett, Allison. "English Teachers' Racial Literacy Knowledge and Practice." *Race, Ethnicity, and Education* 14, no. 3 (2011): 313–30.

Skerrett, Allison, Alisa Adonyi Pruitt, and Amber S. Warrington. "Racial and Related Forms of Specialist Knowledge on English Education Blogs." *English Education* 47, no. 4 (2015): 314–46.

Racial Literacy in Composition Studies

Coleman, Taiyon J., Renee DeLong, Kathleen Sheerin DeVore, Shannon Gibney, and Michael C. Kuhne. "The Risky Business of Engaging Racial Equity in Writing Instruction: A Tragedy in Five Acts." *Teaching English in the Two-Year College* 43, no. 4 (2016): 347–70.

Grayson, Mara Lee. "Race Talk in the College Composition Classroom: Narrative Song Lyrics as Texts for Racial Literacy." *Teaching English in the Two-Year College* 45, no. 2 (2017).

Grayson, Mara Lee. "Racial Literacy in the College Composition Classroom: Developing Discursive Practices through Critical Writing and Textual Analysis." Unpublished doctoral dissertation, Columbia University, New York, 2017.

Johnson, Michelle T. "Race(ing) Around in Rhetoric and Composition Circles: Racial Literacy as the Way Out." Unpublished doctoral dissertation, University of North Carolina, Greensboro, 2009.

Sealey-Ruiz, Yolanda. "Building Racial Literacy in First-Year Composition." *Teaching English in the Two-Year College* (2013): 384–98.

Winans, Amy E. "Cultivating Racial Literacy in White, Segregated Settings: Emotions as Site of Ethical Engagement and Inquiry." *Curriculum Inquiry* 40, no. 3 (2010): 475–91.

Racial Literacy with Pre-College Students

Husband, Terry. "Using Drama Pedagogy to Develop Critical Racial Literacy in an Early Childhood Classroom." *Perspectives and Provocations* 4, no. 1 (2014): 16–51.

King, LaGarrett Jarriel. "Teaching Black History as a Racial Literacy Project." *Race, Ethnicity, and Education* 19, no. 6 (2016): 1303–18.

Rogers, Rebecca, and Melissa Mosley. "Racial Literacy in a Second-Grade Classroom: Critical Race Theory, Whiteness Studies, and Literacy Research." *Reading Research Quarterly* 41, no. 4 (2006): 462–95.

Vetter, Amy, and Holly Hungerford-Kressor. "'We Gotta Change First': Racial Literacy in a High School English Classroom. *Journal of Language and Literacy Education* 10, no. 1 (2014): 82–99.

Racial Literacy in Policy and Administration

Horsford, Sonya Douglas. "When Race Enters the Room: Improving Leadership and Learning through Racial literacy." *Theory into Practice* 53 (2014): 123–30.

Stevenson, Howard C. *Promoting Racial Literacy in Schools: Differences That Make a Difference.* New York: Teachers College Press, 2014.

Critical Whiteness and White Privilege

Beech, Jennifer. "Redneck and Hillbilly Discourse in the Writing Classroom: Classifying Critical Pedagogies of Whiteness." *College English* 67 (2004): 172–86.

Borsheim-Black, Carlin. "'It's Pretty Much White': Challenges and Opportunities of an Anti-racist Approach to Literature Instruction in a Multilayered White Context." *Research in the Teaching of English* 49, no. 4 (2015): 407–29.

DiAngelo, Robin. *What Does It Mean to Be White? Developing White Racial Literacy.* New York: Peter Lang, 2016.

Knowles, Eric D., and Brian S. Lowery. "Meritocracy, Self-Concerns, and Whites' Denial of Racial Inequity." *Self and Identity* 11 (2012): 202–22.

Tatum, Beverly Daniel. "Teaching White Students about Racism: The Search for White Allies and the Restoration of Hope." *Teachers College Record* 95, no. 4 (1994): 462–76.

Personal Writing, Self-Identity, and Composition Pedagogy

Boegeman, Margaret Byrd. "Lives and Literacy: Autobiography in Freshman Composition." *College English* (1980): 662–69.

Denzin, Norman K. *Interpretive Autoethnography.* Los Angeles: Sage, 2014.

Grayson, Mara Lee. "Breathing to Write: Moments of Yoga in First-Year Composition." *Teaching English in the Two-Year College* 44, no. 4 (2017): 450–52.

Gutkind, Lee. *Keep It Real: Everything You Need to Know about Researching and Writing Creative Nonfiction.* New York: Norton, 2008.

Mesquita, Batja. "Emotions Are Culturally Situated." *Social Science Information* 46 (2007).

Moffett, James. "Bridges: From Personal Writing to the Formal Essay." *Center for the Study of Writing* (March 1989).

Ortmeier-Hooper, Christina. "English May Be My Second Language, but I'm Not 'ESL.'" *College Composition and Communication* (2008): 389–419.

Shen, Fan. "The Classroom and the Wider Culture: Identity as a Key to Learning English Composition." *College Composition and Communication* 40, no. 4 (1989): 459–66.

Takacs, David. "How Does Your Positionality Bias Your Epistemology?" *Thought and Action* (2003): 27–38.

Composition Theory and Pedagogy

Blau, Sheridan. "Contexts for Competence in Composition." *The Quarterly* 9, no. 4 (1987): 4–7, 27.

Conference on College Composition and Communication. *Principles for the Postsecondary Teaching of Writing.* Revised March 2015. http://www.ncte.org/cccc/resources/positions/postsecondarywriting.

DasBender, Gita. "Critical Thinking in College Writing: From the Personal to the Academic." In *Writing Spaces: Readings on Writing*, vol. 2, edited by Charles Lowe and Pavel Zemliansky. West Lafayette, IN: Parlor Press, 2011.

Emig, Janet "Writing as a Mode of Learning." *College Composition and Communication* 28, no. 2 (1977): 122–28.

Lindemann, Erika. "Freshman Composition: No Place for Literature." *College English* 55, no. 3 (1993): 311–16.

Teaching of Literature

Appleman, Deborah. "What We Teach and Why: Contemporary Literary Theory and Adolescents." *Minnesota English Journal* 43 (2007).

Blau, Sheridan D. *The Literature Workshop: Teaching Texts and Their Readers.* Portsmouth, NH: Heinemann, 2003.

Blau, Sheridan. "Performative Literacy: The Habits of Mind of Highly Literate Readers." *Voices from the Middle* 10, no. 3 (2003): 18–22.

Graff, Gerald. "Why How We Read Trumps What We Read." *Profession* (2009).

Iser, Wolfgang. *The Act of Reading: A Theory of Aesthetic Response.* Baltimore: Johns Hopkins University Press, 1978.

Paul, Annie Murphy. "Your Brain on Fiction." *New York Times*, March 18, 2012.

Rosenblatt, Louise M. *Literature as Exploration.* 5th ed. New York: Modern Language Association of America, 1995.

Thomas, Ebony Elizabeth. "'We Always Talk about Race': Navigating Race Talk Dilemmas in the Teaching of Literature." *Research in the Teaching of English* 50, no. 2 (2015): 154–75.

Wilhelm, Jeffrey D. *You Gotta Be the Book: Teaching Engaged and Reflective Reading with Adolescents.* 2nd ed. New York: Teachers College Press, 2008.

Media and Music in the English Classroom

Fay, Marion. "Music in the Classroom: An Alternative Approach to Teaching Literature." *Teaching English in the Two-Year College* (2001): 372–78.

Gosa, Travis L., and Tristan G. Fields. "Is Hip-Hop Education Another Hustle? The (Ir)Responsible Use of Hip Hop as Pedagogy." In *Hip-Hop(e): The Cultural Practice and Critical Pedagogy of International Hip-Hop*, edited by Brad J. Porfilio and Michael Viola. New York: Peter Lang, 2012.

Grater, Emily, and Danielle Johnson. "The Power of Song: Cultural Relevance in the Eighth-Grade Classroom." *Voices from the Middle* 22, no. 1 (2013): 32–40.

Hill, Marc Lamont. *Beats, Rhymes, and Classroom Life: Hip-Hop Pedagogy and the Politics of Identity.* New York: Teachers College Press, 2009.

Kellner, Doug, and Jeff Share. "Toward Critical Media Literacy: Core Concepts, Debates, Organizations, and Policy." *Discourse: Studies in the Cultural Politics of Education* 26, no. 4 (2005).

Kelly, Lauren Leigh. "Hip-Hop Literature: The Politics, Poetics, and Power of Hip-Hop in the English Classroom." *English Journal* 102, no. 5 (2013): 51–56.

Levy, Denise L., and Daniel C. Byrd. "Why Can't We Be Friends? Using Music to Teach Social Justice." *Journal of the Scholarship of Teaching and Learning* 11, no. 2 (April 2011): 66–75.

McParland, Robert. "A Sound Education: Popular Music in the College Composition Classroom." In *Teaching in the Pop Culture Zone: Using Popular Culture in the Composition Classroom*, edited by Allison D. Smith, Trixie G. Smith, and Rebecca Bobbitt. Boston: Wadsworth, 2009.

Nakagawa, Kathy, and Angela E. Arzubiaga. "The Use of Social Media in Teaching Race." *Adult Learning* 25, no. 3 (2014): 103–10.

Tatarchevskiy, Tatiana. "The 'Popular' Culture of Internet Activism." *New Media and Society* 13, no. 2 (2011): 297–313.

Social and Cultural Perspectives on Literacy

De Castell, Suzanne, and Allan Luke. "Defining 'Literacy' in North American Schools: Social and Historical Conditions and Consequences." *Journal of Curriculum Studies* 15 (1983): 373–89.

Fairclough, Norman. *Discourse and Social Change.* Cambridge, UK: Polity, 1992.

Freire, Paulo. *Pedagogy of the Oppressed.* 30th anniversary ed. New York: Bloomsbury Academic, 2000.

Teaching in Particular Educational Environments

Emdin, Christopher. *For White People Who Teach in the Hood . . . and the Rest of Y'all Too: Reality Pedagogy and Urban Education.* Boston: Beacon, 2016.

Kynard, Carmen, and Robert Eddy. "Toward a New Critical Framework: Color-Conscious Political Morality and Pedagogy at Historically Black and Historically White Colleges and Universities." *College Composition and Communication* 61, no. 1 (2009): 24–44.

Teiken, Mara Casey. *Why Rural Schools Matter.* Chapel Hill: University of North Carolina Press, 2014.

Trainor, Jennifer Siebel. "The Emotioned Power of Racism: An Ethnographic Portrait of an All-White High School," *College Composition and Communication* 60, no. 1 (2008).

Racial Identity Development

Constantine, Madonna, Tina Q. Richardson, Eric M. Benjamin, and John W. Wilson. "An Overview of Black Racial Identity Theories: Limitations and Considerations for Future Theoretical Conceptualizations." *Applied and Preventive Psychology* 7 (1998): 95–99.

Helms, Janet E. "Toward a Model of White Racial Identity Development." In *Black and White Racial Identity: Theory, Research, and Practice*, edited by Janet E. Helms, 49–66. Westport, CT: Praeger, 1990.

Renn, Kristen A. "Creating and Re-Creating Race: The Emergence of Racial Identity as a Critical Element in Psychological, Sociological, and Ecological Perspectives on Human Development." In *New Perspectives on Racial Identity Development: Integrating Emerging Frameworks*, 2nd ed., edited by Charmaine L. Wijeyesinghe and Bailey W. Jackson III, 11–32. New York: New York University Press, 2012.

Renn, Kristen A. "Patterns of Situational Identity among Biracial and Multiracial College Students." *Review of Higher Education* 23, no. 4 (2000).

Tatum, Beverly Daniel. "Talking about Race, Learning about Racism: The Application of Racial Identity Development Theory in the Classroom." *Harvard Educational Review* 62, no. 1 (1992): 1–24.

RESOURCES FOR STUDENTS

While many of the texts listed here would be fine additions to the racial literacy classroom, especially with more advanced students, the following texts are particularly useful in helping students work through the racial literacy curriculum.

Recognizing Racism

Cobb, Jelani. "The Matter of Black Lives." *New Yorker* 92, no. 5 (2016).

Hodson, Gordon. "Is the 'All Lives Matter' Slogan Racist?" *Psychology Today*, August 25, 2016.

Viney, L-Mani S. "Here's Why It Hurts When People Say 'All Lives Matter.'" *Vanity Fair*, July 19, 2016.

Understanding the Cultural Value of Whiteness

McIntosh, Peggy. "White Privilege: Unpacking the Invisible Knapsack." *Peace and Freedom Magazine* (July/August 1989): 10–12.

Painter, Nell Irvin. "What Is Whiteness?" *New York Times*, June 21, 2015.

Culture, Literacy, and Cultural Literacy

Hirsch, E. D., Jr. *Cultural Literacy: What Every American Needs to Know*. New York: Vintage, 1987.

Liu, Eric. "What Every American Should Know: Defining Common Cultural Literacy for an Increasingly Diverse Nation." *The Atlantic*, July 3, 2015.

Street, Brian. "Culture Is a Verb." In *Language and Culture: Papers from the Annual Meeting of the British Association of Applied Linguistics, Held at Trevelyan College, University of Durham, September 1991*, edited by David Graddol, Linda Thompson, and Mike Byram. Clevedon, UK: British Association for Applied Linguistics in association with Multilingual Matters, 1993.

Conducting Research

Creswell, John W. (2013). *Qualitative Inquiry and Research Design: Choosing among Five Approaches*. 3rd ed. Los Angeles: Sage.

Identity, Positionality, and Personal Writing

Funderburg, Lise. *Black, White, Other: Biracial Americans Talk about Race and Identity*. New York: William Morrow, 1994.

Silverman, Sue William. *Fearless Confessions: A Writer's Guide to Memoir*. Athens: University of Georgia Press, 2009.

ADDITIONAL REFERENCES

Barnhardt, Cassie L. "Campus-Based Organizing: Tactical Repertoires of Contemporary Student Movements." *New Directions for Higher Education* 2014, no. 167 (Fall 2014): 43–58.

Dylan, Bob. "Only a Pawn in Their Game." *The Times They Are a-Changin'*. Columbia Records, 1964.

Foehr, Regina, Miles Myers, Donald R. Gallehr, Richard L. Graves, Sheridan Blau, and Betty Jane Wagner. "A Tribute to James Moffett." *Journal of the Assembly for Expanded Perspectives on Literacy* 3 (1997): 1–12.

Frost, Robert. "The Figure a Poem Makes." In *The Best American Essays of the Century*, edited by Joyce Carol Oates and Robert Atwan. Boston: Houghton Mifflin, 2000.

Gerbaudo, Paolo. *Tweets and the Streets: Social Media and Contemporary Activism*. London: Pluto Press, 2012.

Hairston, Maxine. "The Winds of Change: Thomas Kuhn and the Revolution in the Teaching of Writing," *College Composition and Communication* 33, no. 1 (February 1982): 76–88.

Lave, Jean, and Etienne Wenger. *Situated Learning: Legitimate Peripheral Participation*. Cambridge: Cambridge University Press, 1991.

Mezirow, Jack. "Learning to Think Like an Adult: Core Concepts of Transformation Theory." In *Learning as Transformation: Critical Perspectives on a Theory in Progress*, edited by Jack Mezirow and Associates. San Francisco: Jossey-Bass, 2000.

New York State P–12 Common Core Learning Standards for English Language Arts and Literacy. January 10, 2011. http://schools.nyc.gov/NR/rdonlyres/337BF93A-95FF-4A48-9434 -CE9EA0B70E06/0/p12common_core_learning_standards_ela_final.pdf.

Springsteen, Bruce. "No Surrender." *Born in the U.S.A.* Columbia Records, 1984.

Springsteen, Bruce. "Straight Time." *The Ghost of Tom Joad*. Columbia Records, 1995.

Index

Page references for figures are italicized.

About the Author

Dr. **Mara Lee Grayson** is an educator, researcher, and writer with more than a decade of classroom teaching and tutoring experience. A Brooklyn native, Mara Lee has spent her teaching career in New York City. Currently a lecturer of English at Pace University, she has taught graduate and undergraduate courses in composition, literature, creative writing, technical writing, teacher education, and interdisciplinary studies at Teachers College (Columbia University), City College of New York, LaGuardia Community College, and Long Island University's School of Education. She has also worked with the Poetry Outreach and Urban Scholars organizations. She sits on the board of the Walter K. Hoerning Foundation and serves as secretary and treasurer for the New Jersey College English Association (NJCEA).

Mara Lee earned a PhD in English education from Columbia University and an MFA in creative writing from the City College of New York. She completed undergraduate studies with the Macaulay Honors College at Hunter College, where she learned that education is about far more than the skills we teach inside the classroom. A former staff writer and critic for the theatrical trade paper *Show Business Weekly*, her scholarship, fiction, and poetry have been published in *Teaching English in the Two-Year College*, *Columbia Journal*, *Fiction*, *Construction*, and *Mr. Beller's Neighborhood*, among other publications.

In addition to her work as an English educator, Mara Lee is a yoga teacher (E-RYT-200, RPYT). Whether in the yoga studio or the college classroom, she strives to foster an inclusive environment where each student can enjoy the support of both the community and the room to safely deepen his or her individual practice. Mara Lee lives in Brooklyn with her husband and two cats. She welcomes your correspondence at maraleegrayson@gmail.com.